COLLECTING
POTTERY &
PORCELAIN
The Facts At Your Fingertips

COLLECTING
POTTERY &
PORCELAIN
The Facts At Your Fingertips

General Editor:
Janet Gleeson

Special Consultants:
Keith Baker,
Gordon Lang,
John Sandon &
Lita Solis-Cohen

Collecting Pottery & Porcelain
The Facts At Your Fingertips

First published in Great Britain in 1997 by Miller's, a division of
Mitchell Beazley, imprints of Reed International Books Limited,
Michelin House, 81 Fulham Road, London SW3 6RB
and Auckland and Melbourne

This edition is distributed in the United States by
Antique Collectors Club Ltd.
Market Street Industrial Park, Wappingers' Falls
New York, NY 12590, USA

Executive Editor Alison Starling
Executive Art Editor Vivienne Brar
Project Editor Nina Sharman
Text editor Wendy Lee
Designer Louise Griffiths
Picture Research Jenny Faithfull
Production Jilly Sitford
Special photography Chris Halton, Tim Ridley

The publishers will be grateful for any information that will assist them in
keeping future editions up to date. Although all reasonable care has been
taken in the preparation of this book, neither the publishers nor the
compilers can accept any liability for any consequence arising from the
use thereof, or the information contained herein.

ISBN 1 84000 040 6

A CIP record for this book is available from the British Library

Set in Bembo

Printed and bound in Hong Kong

Front cover *(Top left)* Meissen group of Messetin and Columbine, c.1740, $2,700–3,750. *(Top right)* Coffe cup and saucer, c.1930, $45–60. *(Centre)* Small Wemyss pig, c.1910, $450–600. *(Bottom left)* Blue and white transfer-printed plate by Joseph Stubbs, c.1822–35, $270–360. *(Bottom right)* Clarice Cliff "Avignon" jug, c.1930, $2,100–2,200.
Front flap William de Morgan "Persianware" vase, c.1900, $15,000 or more.
Back cover Böttger Kakiemon flared beaker, c.1725, $1,500–2,750
Back flap Staffordshire spaniel (one of a pair), mid-19thC, $1,650–2,750.

Page 2 *(Top left)* Deruta wet-drug jar, c.1507, $22,500–30,000. *(Top right)* English delft bowl, c.1740, $1,500–2,100. *(Centre left)* Plate from a Meissen dinner service, c.1763–1764, $600–900. *(Centre)* Chinese blue and white vase, early 18thC, $1,950–4,500 depending on size. *(Centre right)* Westerwald blue-glazed jug, late 17thC, $1,800–2,700. *(Bottom left)* Susie Cooper Kestrel-shape teapot, 1930s, $90–135. *(Bottom right)* Staffordshire creamware equestrian group, c.1785, $9,000–15,000.

Page 3 *(Top left)* "Rhodian ware dish late 16thC, $15,000–30,000. *(Top right)* Meissen teapot, c.1745, $4,500–6,000. *(Centre)* Salt-glazed agateware seated cat, c.1745, $1,200–1,800. *(Bottom left)* Red Nicolson vase, late 19th/early 20thC. *(Bottom right)* Staffordshire Toby jug, c.1830, $420–600.

CONTENTS

INTRODUCTION

Browse through any auction or antiques fair catalogue and ceramics of one sort or another will invariably feature prominently. Visually appealing, remarkably diverse, available at an incomparably wide spectrum of prices, pottery and porcelain have long captured the attentions of collectors; and as the world of antiques and collectables in general attracts an ever-growing number of enthusiasts, ceramics seem set to remain as popular as ever.

But what is it about pottery and porcelain that has made them so fascinating to so many people throughout the centuries? In bridging the gap between the useful and the decorative, ceramics provide a fascinating insight into the lifestyle of our forebears, combined with huge aesthetic appeal. Today we may prefer to keep a bleeding bowl or an *albarello* on the dresser rather than collect blood or store chemicals in it, but our enjoyment of such objects is greatly enhanced by an understanding of their origins. Learning how such objects were made and what inspired their decoration is as much a part of collecting as being able to spot the bargains, an aspect on which this book focuses wherever possible.

Clay was used from the earliest times to create functional objects in which man could store and serve food and other essentials. As potters became increasingly adept at using the raw materials available they began adorning their primitive vessels with increasing sophistication, developing coloured pigments to decorate them and glazes to make them water-resistant. The potter's blossoming technical prowess evolved hand in hand with an increasingly sophisticated society, in which there was a demand not only for useful objects but for decorative, prestigious ones as well. So the humble clay pots fashioned by primitive man gave rise to refined clay, stoneware and porcelain objects that were beautiful enough to be regarded as works of art.

The most dramatic development in the history of ceramics came with the development of porcelain in China in the Tang dynasty (618–906AD). When, in the 16th century, Portuguese traders began exporting Chinese porcelain in quantity to the Western world, porcelain objects quickly became highly prized among the affluent few who were able to afford them, and potters in Europe vied continuously with one another for the secret of how to make this magical, translucent substance. Kings and emperors throughout Europe squandered fortunes on endeavouring to discover the secret of making porcelain, and the royal cachet associated with the leading factories that were eventually established at Meissen, Vienna, Sèvres, Copenhagen and St Petersburg helped fuel the public passion for other sophisticated products. Today, as we handle and enjoy these amazingly fragile survivors of the past, their technical and artistic skill remains compelling – little wonder they are as keenly collected as ever.

But with such a dauntingly varied array of subjects from which to choose, how does the new collector know where to begin? Most enthusiasts focus on a particular area, and there are many ways in which the field of ceramics can be broken down into smaller specialities. You could concentrate on ceramics of a particular period and type – such as 17th-century French faience, 18th-century salt-glazed stoneware; transfer-printed ware or 19th-century majolica. Alternatively, you could choose an interesting factory, perhaps Meissen, Wedgwood or Spode. Many other collectors form attractive collections by concentrating on a particular type of ware – say teapots, or coffee cups or saucers.

Traditionally the most popular ceramic collecting areas have been early Oriental ceramics, 17th- and 18th-century European pottery, and 18th-century European porcelain made by famous factories. As prices for these highly prized wares have risen and good examples have become less readily available, collectors have gradually turned their attentions to other less exclusive collecting areas. In recent decades subjects such as blue and white transfer-printed pottery, majolica, or the products of some of the most innovative 20th-century factories and designers, including Carlton, Clarice Cliff, Susie Cooper and Shelley, have seen a huge surge in public interest. The good news for collectors is that, whatever your budget, taste and interests, you are almost certain to find some area of ceramics that fits the bill.

Taking time to learn about your chosen subject is of course one of the best ways to avoid making expensive mistakes, and learning to spot the bargains. This book aims to offer a general introduction to some of the major collecting areas, both traditional and new, and provide you with some historical background along with practical information on what to look for and what prices to expect to pay. Once you have chosen a subject there are a wealth of detailed specialist books on almost every topic covered in this book from which you can expand your knowledge – many are listed on pp168–9. You should also spend time visiting public collections, salerooms and dealers' galleries to examine similar pieces closely before you begin to buy. Remember that simply reading books or looking at pieces in a museum is no substitute for hands-on experience. Ceramics is a three-dimensional art; therefore if you take time to familiarize yourself with the feel and look of the genuine, spotting fakes will be far less difficult. When you visit a dealer or saleroom do not be afraid to pick pieces up and handle them. Look at the body, the appearance of the glaze, the style and colours used in the decoration; consider the weight and any distinctive imperfections. Take the marks into account but do not rely on them entirely as a sign of authenticity. If you do make the odd mistake, bear in mind that you are in good company – most experts have occasionally been fooled, and making mistakes is part of the learning process that all collectors go through.

Whatever collecting area you decide to focus on, value is largely determined by common factors: rarity, size, decorative appeal, popularity and condition are almost invariably critical in establishing the value of any piece of pottery or porcelain. Pieces of unusual form, shape, style or decoration are always appealing to serious collectors and therefore likely to command far higher prices than more readily available wares. Visually appealing pieces are also in keen demand, and the value of pieces made in the 19th and 20th centuries is especially reliant on their decorative appeal. Large pieces are usually more striking than smaller ones and therefore tend to be more valuable. Similarly, pairs or sets of decorative objects, such as vases, appeal to the decorative market and will often cost more than twice the price of a single object. Both pottery and porcelain are inherently fragile, and the value of all types of ceramics is enormously affected by damage. Provenance is yet another factor that can add dramatically to value. Even fairly run-of-the-mill pieces are given extra cachet if they are known to have belonged to a famous person, and labels from well-known collections will always boost value. Fashion and popularity also have a bearing on price. As certain areas enjoy a surge of interest and prices go up others may fall into relative decline.

The categories and objects we have chosen to illustrate in this book are intended to provide an overview of an extraordinarily complex and wide-ranging subject and also to reflect the types of ceramics you are likely to see on the market today. The objects are grouped mainly by type of ware and factory; but in some cases they highlight some of the more popular growing collecting areas such as commemorative ceramics, blue and white, lustre and ironstone. We hope that the varied assortment of information we have included will fire your appetite to learn more about this enthralling subject and that the collection you build as a result will provide you with a source of lasting pleasure – and who knows, perhaps you will even make a profit too.

> The values given in this book for featured objects reflect the sort of prices you might expect to pay for similar pieces at an auction house or from a dealer. As there are so many variable factors involved in the pricing of antiques, the values should be used only as a general guide.

MAIN AREAS OF PRODUCTION
– EUROPE & THE UNITED STATES

European and American pottery and porcelain are generally classified according to the type of ware for example, earthenware, maiolica, faience and stoneware, and the area in which the piece was produced. The map below shows many of the most famous centres of European and American production each of which developed their own distinctive style often drawing on influences from other European centres or from imported Oriental ceramics. In some instances the areas marked refer to a single prominent factory, such as Meissen, Sèvres or Coalport, in others names such as Delft, Moustier or Marseilles denote a region or town in which small manufacturers were grouped, rather than an individual maker.

MAIN AREAS OF PRODUCTION
– CHINA & JAPAN

Pottery and porcelain was produced in China probably earlier than anywhere else. Chinese ceramics are often classified by the area, dynasty and reign in which they were produced. Porcelain was first produced in the north of China during the Tang dynasty. The famous porcelain of the northern Song dynasty (960–1127) comes from Hebei and Henan and is known as Dingyao. Jingdezhen became a centre of ceramic production in the Yuan period and became paramount in the Ming era and remains so today.

Ceramics have been made in Japan since the Neolithic period. The main centre of pottery production was at Seto and the term *Seto-mono* became equivalent to pottery itself. Porcelain was made in Japan from 1616 when a source of china clay was discovered at Arita.

PART 1

BUYING & SELLING

POTTERY & PORCELAIN

ABOVE A MEISSEN FIGURE OF HARLEQUIN FROM THE
COMMEDIA DELL'ARTE, C.1740. $12,000–15,000

LEFT A COLLECTION OF STAFFORDSHIRE FIGURES,
POTTERY AND PORCELAIN FROM THE 19TH CENTURY.

AUCTIONS

Auctions can be one of the most exciting and fruitful ways to buy and sell pottery and porcelain. There is a huge variety of sale-rooms from which to choose. On the one hand you have the larger establishments which divide ceramic sales into categories according to the age and country of origin or type of ware. Specialist categories may include English ceramics, European porcelain, 19th-century ceramics, Art Nouveau, Clarice Cliff, Wedgwood, Staffordshire figures and studio ceram-ics. On the other hand there are numerous smaller firms where ceramics may well be sold alongside furniture and other works of art, or where ceramics of all types are sold together. If you are a novice collector, buying at auc-tion, whether you decide to visit a grand London saleroom or a small country auction house, is not nearly as daunting as it might seem provided you follow a few guidelines.

CATALOGUES

Most salerooms provide a catalogue of the sale that contains a list of the items in the order in which they will be sold. Catalogues vary from glossy publications with colour illustrations and lengthy descriptions, to simple typed sheets. They are available from one month to a week prior to the sale and are worth buying and studying before you visit the saleroom to give you an idea of what is on offer. Most catalogue descrip-tions will state the name of the manufacturer if known, the type of body (materials used), the sort of object, a description of the decoration, a date or approximate date of man-ufacture as well as details of any marks. In some catalogues they also provide information on any damage.

VIEWING

In the days before the sale takes place there will be a "view" at which you can examine the ceramics on offer. It is important always to try and attend the view; do not be tempted to turn up on the morning of the sale and expect to be able to see everything because more often than not the porters will be preparing the lots for the auction and it will be impossi-ble to view properly. Examine anything that catches your eye very, very carefully and make

> **BUYING AT AUCTION CHECKLIST**
> - STUDY THE CATALOGUE
> - VIEW THOROUGHLY
> - STICK TO YOUR LIMIT

The highly charged atomosphere of the saleroom brings added excitement to collecting.

up your own mind as to its authenticity and age. Bear in mind that although most auction house catalogues include a disclaimer stating that their descriptions express only the "opinion" of the cataloguer, they are legally bound by the Trade Descriptions Act. Don't be afraid to handle the objects to look at the marks and for signs of damage or restoration; ask for assistance if need be. Remember to sift through boxes of multiple lots, as this is often where some of the best bargains are to be found. Most of the larger auction houses include estimates in the catalogue to give you some idea of what you can expect to pay for a lot. If there are no estimates in the catalogue they are often pinned up at the view; if not, ask the valuer in charge of the sale what he or she expects the lot will fetch and they will give you some idea based on the reserve price and the level of interest shown during the view. The valuer might also be able to shed more light on the piece you are interested in and give you some idea as to its provenance.

PAYMENT

While you are at the view, find out about procedures for payment and collection if you intend to bid. Some auction houses do not accept credit cards, others will expect cheques to clear before they let you take your purchases away and most will expect you to pay for and collect anything you buy within five working days; if you do not you will often be charged interest and storage. If you cannot attend the sale you can leave a bid with the commissions clerk. The clerk is bound to buy for you as cheaply as possible, but even so it is always best to attend the sale if you can.

BIDDING

Some sales are day-long affairs, and if the lot in which you are interested comes towards the end of the sale you may not want to sit through the whole event. You can find out from a member of staff roughly how quickly the auctioneer sells (usually between 100–120 lots per hour) and work out approximately when you need to arrive.

On the day of the sale you may need to register before you are able to bid. This usually means filling in a form giving details of your name, address and bank. Some salerooms will then issue you with a piece of card with a bidding number on it (sometimes called a paddle) which you hold up if you are successful in your bidding. Before the sale starts decide on your limit and try to stick to it rather than getting carried away in the heat of the moment and regretting it later. Don't forget that on top of the hammer price you will have to add the buyer's commission of between 10 and 15 percent plus taxes.

When the lot on which you want to bid goes under the hammer do not panic if the auctioneer seems to be ignoring you. Many auctioneers only take bids from two people at once; when one drops out that will be your chance to join in.

SELLING

Selling at auction is no more complicated than buying, although you might find taking your prized dinner service or tea set in for inspection and valuation rather nerve-wracking at first. If you intend visiting one of the larger auction houses it is worth phoning ahead to make sure the relevant expert will be available. There is no charge for a verbal over-the-counter valuation (for written valuations see p20) and the expert will often be able to give you a fairly accurate idea of what the piece might make at auction on the spot, although they might need to take it in for further research before deciding finally on the estimate. Remember that the figure they quote is the hammer price; from this the auction house will deduct a commission of around 10 percent, insurance, and photographic charges if the piece is illustrated in the catalogue. If you are selling ceramics of specialist interest you may be advised to wait for a suitable sale. The expert will also advise you on a reserve price (usually on or just below the low estimate), which prevents the lot being sold below market value should the sale turn out to be poorly attended.

DEALERS

Buying pottery and porcelain from a reputable dealer is one of the easiest and user-friendly ways to begin collecting art. Unlike buying at auction you do not have to make up your mind in an instant as to how much you are prepared to pay; in fact some dealers may even let you take things home on approval so you can decide at your leisure whether or not to buy. But how do you know if a particular dealer is "reputable" or not? A good indication of an honest and knowledgeable dealer is one who belongs to a trade association such as the British Antique Dealers Association (BADA) or London and Provincial Antique Dealers Association (LAPADA). In the United States, the National Art & Antiques Dealers' Association (NAADA) and the Art and Antique Dealers League are similar groups. If you see the logo of one of these organizations in a dealer's window it is a sign that he has agreed to adhere to a strict code of practice and that his stock and expertise have been approved by the association's committee.

Once you find a friendly dealer it is worthwhile establishing a rapport with him, since he or she will often look out for special pieces for your collection. Learning from someone with first-hand practical knowledge of a particular subject can save you from making costly mistakes, and a dealer will often give you an insight into the workings of the art market that would be impossible to learn from books and other more conventional sources.

Many general antique shops have odd pieces of pottery or porcelain in stock. Other dealers are more highly specialized and may deal only in ceramics of a certain kind – there are well-known dealers whose stock only includes 18th-century English porcelain, Japanese ceramics, Staffordshire figures, Art Nouveau ceramics or early English pottery. If you are a regular buyer or if you ask to be put on the mailing list of interesting dealers, you may be invited to exhibition previews, which give you the chance to buy before the public at large have seen the goods on offer, and in the case of a contemporary potter this may give you the opportunity to meet the artist in person and discuss his or her work firsthand.

Although buying from specialist dealers has its advantages, do not ignore the less specialist sources. The more recently popular ceramics can still be found for very modest sums. Hidden in a local house clearance emporium you may discover a highly desirable Doulton figure or a stylish piece of Susie Cooper, and you will probably pay less for it than you would in a specialist's shop. However, if you buy from such sources you cannot expect the same level of guidance that you would receive in a specialist shop.

If you are buying the work of a relatively well-known pottery do try and price pieces in more than one source before you make an expensive purchase. Useful sources of reference include the annual *Miller's Antiques Price Guide* which publishes prices of ceramics sold at auction and in dealers' galleries along with a brief description. Bear in mind that although the price of a work of art at auction may well be lower than if you buy from a dealer, the dealer may well have paid to restore the piece to a high standard, and unlike buying at auction, when you buy from a dealer there are no other costs such as buyer's commission.

BUYING FROM A DEALER OR GALLERY

When you have some idea of the market value of the ceramics of your choice, don't haggle aggressively but do ask the dealer for his "best price" – you may be pleasantly surprised by a small discount. Before you buy ask the dealer as many questions as you can about the piece that has caught your eye. If possible find out where he bought it, because a good

---

BUYING FROM A DEALER CHECKLIST
- CHOOSE A REPUTABLE DEALER
- ASK QUESTIONS ABOUT THE OBJECTS
- GET A DETAILED RECEIPT

provenance adds to value. Has it been heavily restored? Are the marks "right"? Once you have paid make sure you are given a receipt with the dealer's name, trading address and a full description of the piece, including the name of the manufacturer if known, type of ware, date or approximate date of manufacturer and the price paid. Keep the receipt in a safe place as it will be useful for insurance purposes, and in the unlikely event as to there being a later dispute over authenticity.

"KNOCKERS"
Avoid selling to people who call unsolicited at your home, or put a note through your door asking whether you have any "antiques" for sale. Many of these so-called "knockers" are highly unscrupulous people whose aim is to trick you into parting with your property for much less than it is worth.

SELLING TO A DEALER
Eye-catching headlines about works of art that sell for thousands of dollars at auction can give the misleading impression that selling in the saleroom is more profitable than selling direct to a dealer. Contrary to popular belief this is not always the case, and as with buying there can be significant advantages to selling to a dealer. In the first place, the sum you agree with the dealer is the sum you will actually receive; there are no other deductions, such as seller's commission, photographic charges and insurance. If you agreed, say, to sell a vase for $750 to a dealer, you would receive exactly that amount. Sell a vase at auction for the same hammer price and you will receive (after several weeks) a cheque for around $630 (assuming commission at 12½ percent, 1 percent insurance and sales taxes); photographic charges would reduce the figure further.

Before you sell to a dealer it is always worth checking the value of your property with more than one person. The public nature of an auction room means that even if the cataloguer has under-valued your property the chances are that it will still realize its market value. When you sell to a dealer you have no

Ceramics on display at a specialist dealer's gallery.

such safeguard so it is wise to seek more than one opinion before you agree a final figure. Always try to sell to a specialist in the type of ware you are offering. An expert in Chinese ceramics will have a better knowledge of the current values of, say, a Canton jardinière than a general antiques dealer and so is more likely to offer you a realistic price.

If the collection you want to sell is large, or the piece fragile and difficult to transport, showing dealers a photograph is a good way of gauging interest and avoiding inadvertent damage. Most dealers will not charge for a verbal valuation and many will visit your home to save you from moving the pieces.

FAIRS & MARKETS

Apart from buying at auction or a dealer's gallery there are numerous other places in which you can find pottery and porcelain to add to your collection. There are street markets such as Portobello Road, Camden Lock and Bermondsey in London and the famous *Marché aux Puces* in Paris which take place on one or two days every week and where dealers in a wide variety of art and antiques congregate to sell their wares. At these large markets you will find a combination of shops, covered stalls and some stalls that are no more than a trestle table on the street. Not surprisingly you are likely to come across an equally wide cross-section of dealers at a street fair; some of them will be members of trade associations, others will not, and while the unpopular English law of *marché ouvert*, which facilitated the legal sale of stolen property at markets, has now been changed, it is still up to you to satisfy yourself as to the dealer's integrity.

Large annual antiques shows have enjoyed a huge rise in popularity in recent years and can be one of the most appealing and safe ways for novice collectors to buy. You can buy a wide range of antiques and collectables at some of the large regular fairs (see pp164–5). There are also fairs which focus solely on pottery and porcelain. Most of the larger fairs are advertised in the national press and in specialist publications.

If you are unsure of what type of ceramics you want to collect a large fair is an ideal starting place since you have a concentration of dealers all assembled under one roof, offering a wide selection of pottery and porcelain. In addition, you often find unusual and rare pieces are exhibited for the first time at major fairs. Many dealers invest considerable sums of money in taking a stand at one of the large fairs so they will often "hold back" prize objects to make their stand more appealing.

The wide choice of dealers at specialist fairs also gives you a golden opportunity to compare prices of similar types of ware without wearing out your shoe-leather. Another advantage that most of the larger prestigious fairs offer is the added safeguard of a vetting committee. "Vetting" means that every piece of pottery or porcelain on a dealer's stand will have been examined and approved as authentic by a panel of independent experts. Some vetted fairs also operate a "dateline", which means that only pieces before a given date, say 1890, are eligible to be sold.

Most large fairs charge an entrance fee which may include the cost of a catalogue of exhibitors. These publications contain the business addresses and telephone numbers of

---

> **BUYING CHECKLIST AT FAIRS & MARKETS**
> - COMPARE PRICES AND STOCK AT SEVERAL STALLS
> - BE THERE EARLY TO FIND THE BEST BARGAINS
> - TRY TO GET A RECEIPT

Fairs and flea markets are often a fertile source of bargains for keen collectors.

Hopeful buyers at a local flea market.

all the exhibitors and are a useful future source of reference to locate reputable dealers even if you don't buy from them at the fair. Provided a dealer lives within easy travelling distance of your home, don't forget that if you spot something that catches your eye but can't quite make up your mind, you can always visit the dealer after the fair at his or her premises to view the stock in a more leisurely fashion. Many dealers regard fairs as an essential method of contacting new collectors and are only too happy for you to visit them later, although there is of course no guarantee that they won't have sold the object you liked.

SMALLER FAIRS

There is a world of difference between these large, professionally organized events and the plethora of smaller antiques and collectors' fairs that take place in such diverse venues as church halls, schools and even car parks. Fairs of this type are usually advertised in the local press; you may pay an entrance fee to get in to them but there is generally no catalogue, no vetting committee and no guarantee of the

authenticity of the goods on offer. It is therefore up to you to decide whether what you see is worth the money you are asked for it.

FLEA MARKETS

Flea markets have attracted huge attention recently as without fail each year a handful of hitherto unrecognized heirlooms are bought for a few pence and later sold for tens of thousands of pounds. Like smaller fairs, flea markets are held in a wide variety of venues, including car parks and farmers' fields, and are usually advertised in the local press. Although the chances of finding a very valuable object are, realistically, pretty remote, modest bargains are not unusual, and they can be good places to buy 20th-century ceramics for reasonable sums. The best way to find a bargain at a flea market is to turn up early and to remember to take a torch if it's winter and the light is poor. Dealers are always first on the scene, sifting through the contents of cardboard boxes and tea chests as they are unpacked. If you can beat them to it you stand a good chance of finding something interesting and unusual that might just turn out to be more valuable than you expected.

PART 2

CARING FOR YOUR
COLLECTION

ABOVE CLARICE CLIFF TEAPOT C.1935.
$600–900

LEFT AN ASSORTMENT OF BLUE AND WHITE
PORCELAIN ATTRACTIVELY DISPLAYED ON WALL
BRACKETS ABOVE A CHIMNEYPIECE.

SECURITY

One of the less pleasant aspects of collecting any type of antique is the increasing risk of theft. As the incidence of theft and burglary steadily rises it has never been more important to protect and insure your collection properly. Theft is the biggest single risk to antique collections and currently accounts for around 60 percent of all insurance claims for art; fire, the next single biggest risk, is responsible for around 25 percent of art claims.

Nevertheless the news is not all bad. If you are unlucky enough to be burgled a thief is far less likely to help himself to your antiques than your CD player or video, which are much easier for the average burglar to dispose of. Among the various antique collecting fields, silver, jewellery and small clocks and watches are the most portable and obviously valuable, hence are most vulnerable to theft. If you need help in choosing the best way of protecting your collection contact your local police department who will give you advice and recommend reputable security firms. Although ceramics are more vulnerable to accidental damage than many other types of antique, thefts are still relatively rare. For this reason, provided you are prepared to shop around, you should be able to insure your collection at reasonable cost.

> **SECURITY CHECKLIST**
> - **MAKE YOUR HOME SECURE**
> - **PHOTOGRAPH VALUABLES BUT DO NOT KEEP THE PHOTORAPHS IN YOUR HOME**
> - **KEEP AN INVENTORY OF YOUR COLLECTION**

INSURING

If you have only a handful of relatively inexpensive pieces you may find it is most practical to include them on your general household contents policy. If on the other hand the value of your collection amounts to more than about $75,000 it would almost certainly be worth your while to insure with a specialist firm. (If they are worth $37,500–75,000 you should investigate both options.) The advantage of dealing with a specialist firm is that the various risks associated with different types of antique are reflected in lower premiums.

Specialist firms may have an annual charge of as little as 50¢ per $150 insured for antiques whereas if you include art in a general policy you may pay at least twice as much. The disadvantage of dealing with a specialist firm is that they are not really interested in smaller collections and many have minimum premiums of around $750 per year.

VALUATIONS

Once you have shopped around to find the best insurance policy, you will probably find the insurance company requires a written valuation of the ceramics (and any other objects) in your collection. Most auction houses have departments that undertake insurance valuations; there are also specialist valuers (many of them auction house-trained) or you can also try a reputable local dealer.

Valuations are well worth having because in the event of a claim a recent valuation by a reputable source will make disputes with the insurance company over the value of an item less likely. When you take an object to an auction house or dealer for an informal valuation there is no charge, but you can expect to pay for a written insurance valuation. Once again

Over-the-counter valuations are normally free, but a fee will usually be charged for written insurance valuations.

costs vary widely and it is worth shopping around to compare prices.

As a general guide there are three ways in which valuations can be priced: firstly, as a percentage of the sum insured, usually between ½ and 1½ percent. Unless you only need a valuation for one or two items this is usually the most expensive way to pay. Secondly, the charges may be based on how long it takes a valuer to assess your property. As a rule a well-qualified valuer will be able to catalogue and value around 100–300 objects a day. Finally, you may find you can agree a fixed rate for the valuation.

Whichever method you opt for, remember to negotiate before the valuation is made. Make sure whoever you select for the job is properly qualified and has sufficient expertise in the subject or you may find, in the event of a claim, it is impossible to replace something for the specified amount. If, say, you have a highly specialized collection of early English pottery you would be well advised to use a company with an expert in the field (such as a larger auction house) rather than consulting a general ceramics dealer who may have little knowledge of current market prices.

Whoever you choose for the job, make sure that the valuation is acceptable to the insurer. The valuation document should include a full description of the object. In the case of ceramics this would involve the maker, the type of object, the material (earthenware, porcelain, stoneware etc.), the date or approximate date, the size (height before width) and the value for insurance purposes.

Before the valuer begins you should agree with him the level of the valuation. This depends largely on where you would go to replace the objects in the event of their loss. Would you go shopping in an expensive city gallery or at a local auction room? Obviously the higher the sum placed on a piece, the more expensive it will be to insure, but at the very least the figure should be about 20 percent more than what you would expect to get should you sell at auction, in order to allow for auction house commissions. Don't forget that if you under-insure you could find yourself unable to replace lost items satisfactorily.

SECURITY

The vast majority of household burglaries are opportunistic and you can reduce the likelihood of a break-in by making your home as uninviting to burglars as possible. Local crime prevention officers will give you free advice on the best security measures to take. Good locks on doors, windows and security lights are all useful deterrents and if an alarm is necessary don't forget that the cost of installing it can often be offset by a reduction in insurance premiums – so make sure you tell your insurance company if you decide to install one.

STOLEN PROPERTY

One of the fundamental ways in which art and antiques differ from electronic equipment, however valuable, is that for many collectors art holds not only commercial but also sentimental value and very often a cheque is a poor substitute for the loss of a much-loved piece of pottery or porcelain. In the unfortunate event of theft there are, however, several measures you can take to help recover your stolen property; all of them depend on having photographs of the missing objects.

The police have a computer database run by the Art and Antiques Squad into which details of stolen objects can be entered to give police throughout the country instant information on such property. The Art Loss Register is another computerized database containing details of stolen property to which dealers, auctioneers and insurance companies subscribe. Dealers and auction houses use the system to check that objects they are offered are not stolen. The cost of including a stolen object on the register is around $30 and the success rate is impressive. There are also specialist publications which can help you trace stolen property. *Trace*, a British magazine in which you can place photographs of stolen property, is distributed nationally and internationally to auction houses and dealers. *IFAR Reports* is a similar publication in the United States.

DISPLAY, CARE & RESTORATION

Of all types of antiques ceramics are among the most vulnerable to damage. If you have recently bought an old piece of pottery or porcelain, it may well have cracks or chips and you may wonder how much, if any, restoration it requires. Modern technology has resulted in the development of restoration techniques of extraordinary effectiveness; not only is it now possible to repair cracked and broken objects with the use of new adhesives, it is also possible to replace even large missing areas with a body that will almost match that of the original.

In the case of serious damage the extent of the restoration is, however, a matter of opinion and something that is worth discussing at length with a skilled restorer. In general the modern approach to restoration favours keeping work to a minimum and avoiding respraying the surface to disguise repairs at the expense of the original decoration.

RESTORATION, HANDLING & DISPLAY CHECKLIST

- USE A PROFESSIONAL RESTORER
- AGREE ON THE COST AND HOW MUCH RESTORATION YOU WANT BEFORE THE WORK BEGINS
- REMOVE LIDS BEFORE HANDLING
- DO NOT LIFT PIECES BY HANDLES
- MAKE SURE HOLDERS AND STANDS ARE THE CORRECT SIZE AND SECURELY FITTED

Always use professional restorers. Restoration is a highly skilled art; an unqualified restorer can cause untold damage to a precious piece of pottery or porcelain and greatly reduce its value. You can find a local qualified restorer through one of the various trade associations (see p164). The restorers that are registered with one of these organizations are professionally qualified and will advise you on the necessary conservation and restoration of your purchase as well as help you to care for it correctly once you take it home.

CLEANING CERAMICS

Any type of ceramic on open display is bound to build up a residue of dirt and dust over time; and while this may not threaten the well-being of the object it is obviously unsightly and needs to be dealt with periodically. Different types of ceramic bodies need to be cleaned in various ways. Although hard-paste porcelain and

Restoring damaged ceramics using modern resin adhesives and enamels.

Modern restoration techniques and adhesives mean that ceramics can be restored increasingly effectively.

high-fired stonewares, despite their apparent fragility, may safely be washed by hand in mild soapy water (unless they have been restored), unglazed ceramics, however, should not normally be exposed to water and should only be dusted. The body of most unglazed ceramics is porous and if you wash them the dirt will soak into the body and cause discoloration. Low-fired earthenwares and other soft-paste types of porcelain and bone china may also be discoloured and damaged by washing, but may usually be wiped gently with a damp cloth. If in doubt about how to deal with a certain type of ceramic do not be afraid to consult a specialist dealer or restorer for advice.

HANDLING CERAMICS

There is no doubt that damage is most likely to occur while ceramics are being handled. However, examining pieces "hands on" is an essential part of learning about them and enjoying them and provided you observe a few simple guidelines there should be no need to feel nervous. When picking up objects with lids, for example, teapots or covered vases, always remove the lid first, preferably without picking it up by the knop which is vulnerable to damage and may be insecure. Lift hollow objects by supporting the body gently using two hands; do not pick up pieces by their handles – again these are often weakened by use. When replacing an object after examining it put it down gently, well away from any other objects on the surface. Try to avoid touching gilding which is easily rubbed and worn through handling.

DISPLAY

However beautiful a piece of pottery or porcelain is, if it is poorly displayed you will considerably diminish its impact. In order to display ceramics effectively they usually need to be securely supported, and placed somewhere they can be enjoyed – out of the way of danger from accidental knocks.

Old plates are often bought with rusty wire hangers still in position; these are an extremely undesirable method of display – as well as being unreliable, they can exert excessive pressure on the body, causing cracks and chips. Remove wire hangers by cutting through the metal on the reverse. Do not attempt to bend the wire from the front as this can chip the rim. If you wish to hang plates or dishes on a wall the best method is to use an acrylic hanger; these are transparent, adjustable and do not have any sharp points that could scratch the surface of the dish. Modern plastic-covered wire hangers in the correct size are suitable for more robust types of ceramics since they have spring adjustments which mean they will not press too tightly on the body. If you wish to display ceramics such as bowls, cups and saucers, dishes or plates on a flat surface like a cabinet shelf or a table, there is also a range of extremely well-designed acrylic stands; again it is imperative that the stand should be exactly the right size to give proper support. Whichever method of display you choose make sure that the ceramics are well protected from vibrations which can cause them to move and fall down or knock into one another.

COLOUR

POTTERY COLOURS

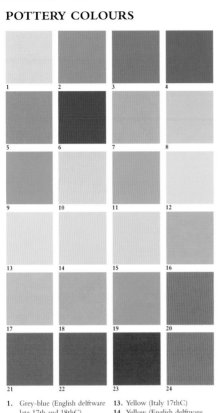

PORCELAIN COLOURS

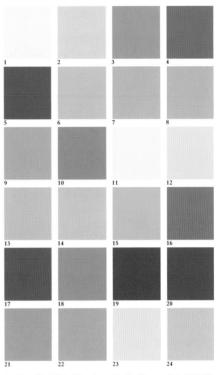

Pottery Colours Key

1. Grey-blue (English delftware late 17th and 18thC)
2. Turquoise (Iznik, Turkey mid-16th–end 17thC)
3. Mid-blue (English delftware late 17th and 18thC)
4. Mid-range cobalt (Venice and Urbino *istoriati*, Italy 16thC)
5. Deep blue (Faenza, Italy c.1525–50)
6. Dark blue (Nevers, France 1650–1700)
7. Greyish-cobalt (Deruta, Italy c.1520–50)
8. Turquoise (Italy late 15thC, English delftware 17thC)
9. Green-blue (Urbino *istoriato*, Italy c.1525–75)
10. Grey-green (Castelli, Siena, Italy 18thC)
11. Grey-green (English delftware 18thC)
12. Yellow-green (Urbino, Italy c.1520–50)
13. Yellow (Italy 17thC)
14. Yellow (English delftware late 17th and 18thC)
15. Ochre (Deruta, Italy c.1500–25)
16. Ochre (Holland early 17thC)
17. Sienna (Deruta, Siena, Italy early 16thC)
18. "Sealing wax red" (Iznik, Turkey mid-16th–end 17thC)
19. Lustre (Spain 15th–16thC)
20. Ruby lustre (Gubbio, Italy c.1500–55)
21. Red (France, Holland, London 18thC)
22. Puce "purple manganese" (Strasbourg, France c.1750–1800)
23. Manganese brown (Italy, Spain 15th–16thC)
24. Stone (Urbino, Italy c.1525–75)

Porcelain Colours Key

1. Misty blue (China Yingqing ·12th–14thC)
2. Turquoise (Meissen c.1740–70, Derby c.1770)
3. *Bleu céleste* (Sèvres, from 1753)
4. Persian blue (Chinese 16thC)
5. Dark cobalt (Ming & Qing 14th–18thC)
6. Turquoise (Chelsea Gold Anchor period)
7. Emerald green (Bow 1660–1770)
8. Apple green (Worcester c.1770, Sèvres c.1756)
9. Early Meissen green (1720–40)
10. Brunswick green (English factories, early 19thC)
11. Lemon-yellow (Meissen c.1730–50)
12. Egg yolk (16thC Chinese)
13. Brownish yellow (Arita, c.1650–1700, late Ming *wucai*)
14. Tan (German, Swiss 1760–70)
15. Rich terracotta (English Neo-classical wares)
16. Russet (Fürstenberg c.1760–70)
17. Dark brown (German 18thC)
18. Iron-red (All factories)
19. Purple (Meissen, 1740s)
20. Claret (Vienna 19thC)
21. English puce (Longton Hall 1749–60)
22. Puce (German factories, mid-18thC)
23. *Rose Pompadour* (from c.1757)
24. Lilac (Meissen, 1750s)

The colours or enamels with which pieces of pottery or porcelain are decorated provide an important clue as to their date and place of origin. Certain colours are associated with particular factories; others were enormously fashionable at a particular time. Rare colours can add greatly to the value of a particular piece. The colours shown above are an approximation of the most common colours used by certain manufacturers and the key gives an indication of when and where they were mostly used.

PART 3

IDENTIFICATION

ABOVE A BERLIN GOLD GROUND CABINET CUP AND
SAUCER C.1820. $4,500–6,000

CLASSIFICATION

Ceramics are primarily classified by the type of body – the materials – from which they are made, and secondly by the type of glaze used. The body of a glazed piece can usually be seen on the base; on most pieces the glaze does not entirely cover the footrim but leaves the underlying body partly visible.

BODY

The materials from which ceramics are made can be broadly divided into three families:

Pottery Made from an earthenware body. Depending on the minerals the clay contains, pottery may be white, buff, brown, red, grey or black in colour; it is coarser in texture than porcelain and the body is opaque.

Stoneware A fine water-resistant body created by firing clays at a high temperature. Some stonewares are slightly translucent and can sometimes resemble porcelain.

Porcelain A mixture of china clay and petuntse (hard paste), or crushed glass or quartz and white clay (soft paste). It is a fine material, that gives a musical note if gently tapped, and may be semi-translucent if held to the light.

POTTERY

The earliest ceramics were made from earthenware, that is, clay fired at a relatively low

English delft flower tub c.1690 – an example of English tin-glazed earthenware pottery. $3,750–5,250

Doulton stoneware jugs made c.1870. $170–375 each

temperature of under 2,200°F (1,200°C). Unglazed earthenware is porous and in order to hold liquids has to be glazed. The types of earthenware commonly seen today include Islamic pottery, Italian and Spanish maiolica, French and German faience, delftware, slipware, Whieldon ware, Staffordshire pottery, creamware, Prattware, pearlware and majolica.

STONEWARE

First used by ancient Chinese potters of the Shang dynasty, stoneware was made from a type of clay that could withstand firing to temperatures of 2,500°F (1,400°C). At these high temperatures components of the clay melted, forming a water-resistant body that was extremely robust. Western stoneware was independently developed in Germany in the Middle Ages. There are two distinct types of stoneware: the first is a fine, white-bodied variety like Sieburg and later Staffordshire. The second, a grey-bodied ware sometimes covered in brown salt glaze which looks pitted like an orange skin, was produced in Cologne, Westerwald and Fulham, London.

PORCELAIN

Porcelain bodies are broadly divided into two categories: hard paste and soft paste. Familiarity with the different types of body can help identify unmarked pieces.

Hard-paste porcelain Has a smooth texture resembling icing sugar. First discovered by ancient Chinese potters hard-paste porcelain was subsequently made by Meissen in Germany and in other European factories throughout the 18th century.

Soft-paste porcelain Is slightly more granular and chips may have a rougher appearance compared to hard paste. Developed in Italy from the 16th century in an attempt to replicate true Oriental porcelain, the colour of the soft-paste body varies between pure white and grey, depending on the minerals used. Colour can also help with identification since certain factories are associated with bodies of a particular shade.

BONE CHINA

Bone china was supposedly developed by Josiah Spode at the end of the 18th century. It is a less expensive method of porcelain making containing calcified bone and is the most commonly found type of porcelain made in England after c.1820; it was produced by Spode, Derby, Rockingham, Coalport, Minton and others. The body of objects made from bone china is pure white in appearance.

GLAZES

Glazes are used to make a porous body watertight and also to decorate a piece. They may be translucent, opaque or coloured. A variety of different glazes were used, each identifiable by its distinctive characteristics.

POTTERY GLAZES

On pottery there are three main types of glaze: lead, tin and salt.

Lead glaze Used on most European earthenwares including creamware and pearlware

as well as Chinese Tang ware. Lead glaze is transparent and shiny in appearance and may be coloured with metal oxides.

Tin glaze A glaze containing tin oxide which gives an opaque white appearance. Tin glaze is found on maiolica, faience and Delftware where it was used to give the earthenware body a pure white finish resembling porcelain. Tin glaze was applied to the fired body, which was then decorated with enamels, and finally coated with clear lead glaze before the piece was returned to the kiln for refiring.

Salt glaze A method commonly used for stoneware where salt was thrown into the kiln during firing at a high temperature. The sodium in the salt fused with silicates in the clay to form a glassy surface. Salt-glazed wares were made in Germany, England as well as the United States. Some salt glaze has a distinctive pitted surface (see p26), which can be a help with identification.

Bow soft-paste porcelain figures of New Dancers
1760–1765. $3,750–5,250

PORCELAIN GLAZES

Glazes on porcelain vary according to the factory concerned and often have a highly distinctive appearance ranging from matt to glassy, opaque to translucent. Glazes can also give porcelain a characteristic tinge of colour; some glazes appear to be pure white while others can seem bluish, yellowish, greyish or greenish in appearance.

Hard paste The glaze typically has a glassy thin appearance.

Soft paste The glaze typically is thicker, softening detailed modelling and pooling in the curves and crevices of a piece.

MARKS

Throughout the centuries ceramics have been marked by their manufacturers and these marks can provide useful information about the maker. Many factories such as Sèvres, Chelsea and Derby changed their marks throughout their long histories and these changes can also help with dating a piece. There are numerous specialist publications available (see pp168–9) that will provide you with invaluable detailed information about the marks in your particular collecting field.

SPURIOUS MARKS

Marks cannot always however be taken at face value. In Chinese ceramics pieces were frequently marked with earlier reign marks as a sign of respect for the skill of earlier potters. The famous Meissen crossed swords mark was imitated by numerous factories throughout Europe; Worcester's crescent mark was also used by Bow; and numerous other factories capitalized on the popularity of successful factories by copying designs and imitating marks.

TYPES OF FACTORY MARK

Marks found on ceramics commonly include a factory mark. This may be a symbol, such as the anchor of Chelsea; initials, monograms and letters, such as the letter "Z" used by the Zurich factory; or the name of the factory written as a word or signature: Minton for example is marked in this way. Marks may be applied to a piece in a variety of different ways: they may be painted by hand in underglaze or overglaze enamels, incised by hand, impressed with a stamp, or printed.

OTHER MARKS

Other marks on ceramics may refer to the various individuals involved:
● the designer
● the decorator
● the modeller (in the case of figures)
● the gilder.
There may also be a pattern serial number which provides useful information when the factory's records have survived.

PRINTED MARKS

Printed marks were used by most major English factories of the 19th century. Small changes in the wording can help with dating:
● From c.1820 – marks with a royal coat of arms began to be seen
● From c.1896 – marks with the word "England" or other country's names, following the McKinley Tariff Act of 1891
● 20th century – marks with the words "Made in England", or "Bone china".

REGISTRATION MARKS

A diamond registration mark was used on English ceramics between 1842 and 1883; letters and numbers in the corners of the diamond refer to the date of manufacture. After 1883 "Rd No" (the registered number) followed by the number itself was used.

FAKES AND COPIES

Copies and imitations of earlier styles have been made throughout the centuries. Most early imitations were not intended to deceive but show admiration for earlier designs. Deliberate faking with the intention to mislead started in the 18th century with the decoration of Sèvres porcelain blanks by independent

A Samson rabbit tureen c.1900, imitating a Chelsea Red Anchor original. $1,500–2,250

decorators who marked them as though they were genuine Sèvres. During the 19th century many imitations of earlier pieces were made, often honestly marked by their maker.

EDMÉ SAMSON
The most prolific imitator of early ceramics, Samson made copies of Oriental, German, French and English ceramics from the mid-19th century. Much of Samson's output was marked with an entwined or squared "S", crossed batons or the "Worcester" seal mark. As values have risen in the 20th century these imitations have become collectable in their own right. Problems arise when unscrupulous dealers remove the Samson mark.

ORIENTAL CERAMICS
● Imitation "Tang" pieces were produced in the early 20th century after the genuine pieces became more widely available following excavations in China. The honest marks on reproductions were often removed by dealers at a later date.
● Imitation pieces were made in the Far East from c.1920; these are sometimes identifiable by heavy potting and poor-quality calligraphy.
● Emil Samson, son of Edmé, made good-quality copies of later Chinese and Japanese porcelain, usually marked with a distinctive square-shaped "S".

ITALIAN POTTERY
● Many copies and fakes of Italian maiolica were made in the 19th century; these are sometimes identifiable by their loosely painted margins, or by overly important borders painted in colours that are too bright.
● The Cantagalli factory made numerous imitations of early Italian pottery and marked them with a cockerel.

GERMAN CERAMICS
● Earlier stoneware styles were revived in the 19th century – copies are discernible by their flat rather than concave bases.
● Copies of 18th-century Meissen were made throughout the 19th century by

The Cantagalli factory mark found on late 19th- and 20th-century imitation maiolica and Iznik ware.

Samson and others; wares were also imitated by minor factories in the 18th century.
● Samson's glaze is often too glassy and smooth and the modelling lacks definition.

FRENCH CERAMICS
● Copies of French faience were made in the 19th century – sometimes identifiable by their stiffly painted decoration.
● Nantgarw produced imitations of French-style porcelain in the early 19th century, but these are highly collectable.
● Coalport and Minton made imitations, mainly of larger Sèvres pieces.
● Many small Paris makers made imitation Sèvres in the 19th century, often with spurious marks.
● Copies of Chantilly and St Cloud were made in hard paste by the Samson factory and others in the late 19th century.

ENGLISH CERAMICS
● Elaborate slipware has been faked at least since the 1920s. Stoneware owl jugs have recently been faked. Look for signs of wear.
● Copies of early stoneware and agateware were produced in the 1920s.
● 19th-century animal tureens imitating Chelsea were made by Samson.
● Worcester's 18th-century wares were copied in Paris in the 19th century.
● Some of Derby's ornamental wares were copied by the Samson factory.

PART 4

CERAMIC FILE

ABOVE A 19TH-CENTURY JARDINIÈRE BY WILLIAM
MOORCROFT IN THE CORNFLOWER PATTERN.
$6,000–9,000

LEFT A COLOURFUL ASSORTMENT OF 19TH CENTURY
ENGLISH POTTERY AND PORCELAIN CAN MAKE AN
EYE-CATCHING DISPLAY.

Isolated from the rest of the world, China was responsible for almost every major development in pottery and porcelain, and throughout the centuries Chinese ceramics have exerted a profound influence over those made in the Far East, Middle East and Europe.

The earliest wares evolved between c.3000 and 1500BC in the Neolithic cultures of the Shandong Peninsula, the Gansu corridor and elsewhere. The pieces that have survived were made as funerary objects and were unglazed and simply decorated with pigments derived from the earth.

During the Shang dynasty (1700–1027BC, China's first historic period, pottery became more and more refined and shapes were based on those of metal artefacts made at the same time. The first lead and feldspathic glazes were not developed until the Han dynasty (206BC–220AD), when high-fired stonewares were made. By the Tang dynasty (618–906AD), commerce and culture began to make themselves felt in the development of ceramics. Outside influences from central Asia gradually infiltrated China, altering the appearance of ceramics, and Chinese wares began to spread throughout the Middle East carried by Arab traders. Potters rediscovered white clay which led ultimately to the development of porcelain.

Considering the great age and historical importance of these early ceramics they are still available at relatively modest prices. Yue wares from the Han dynasty are available from $450–750 and celadon from the Yuan dynasty can also be comparatively inexpensive.

EARLY CHINESE POTTERY

There are few extant examples of pottery made before the Han dynasty (206BC–220AD). A surprising number of Han funerary pottery wares have survived. These were made to accompany the deceased person to the after-life. They are highly stylized and primitively modelled and include figures, animals, models of buildings and vessels. During the Tang dynasty figures became increasingly refined and naturalistically modelled; some objects were unglazed, others were decorated with pigment or straw-coloured glaze, or polychrome glaze known as *sancai* (three-coloured glaze). Horses and camels, are among the most sought-after objects made at this time. Unglazed or straw-glazed figures tend to be less expensive than those with three-coloured glaze.

▲ **FUNERARY JARS**
This jar made in the Neolithic Yangshao culture is decorated with simple black and red pigment and the swirling pattern with chequered roundels is typical of this type. The lower part was left undecorated because the jar would have been partly sunk in earth in the tomb. Incredibly, jars of this type, made nearly 4,000 years ago, are not particularly rare and the value would only be $1,800–2,700.

WHAT TO LOOK FOR

Examine the glaze carefully for signs of authenticity. Points to note are:
- translucent glaze that shows imperfections in the body beneath
- crackling in the glaze
- unevenness – the glaze usually pulls to the base
- an element of iridescence caused by being buried in the soil.

▶ MODEL BUILDINGS

Models of contemporary buildings were usually included in tombs; this is a watchtower made in the Han dynasty. Other buildings you might find from this period include: storehouses, barns, well-heads, gatehouses and granaries. This is quite large (13⅓in [34cm] high) and therefore worth $3,000–4,500; smaller objects cost from $450.

◀ TANG POTTERY

A heavy baluster jar from the Tang dynasty (618–906); the heavy form and small rim are typical characteristics of this period and the decoration is created in a similar way to tie-dye in a standard palette of greens, brown and white. $12,000–15,000

BEWARE

Fakes of horses of this type abound and have been made since the 1920s. The best fakes can be difficult for novice collectors to identify – handling the genuine article is the best way to learn to spot them.

▶ HORSES

Figures such as this unglazed horse were made in the Tang dynasty from different sections: the neck, legs and rump were all probably separately moulded and then joined together. Value depends primarily on the impact of the object. Figures should be crisply modelled and powerful; unusual poses can also greatly add value. This is a conventional pose and unglazed, but still worth $3,750–5,250; if the horse had a foot raised or was slightly rearing it would be far more valuable.

CHINESE STONEWARES

Stoneware is made by firing clay at very high temperatures (2,500°F (1,400°C) and above) during which process part of the clay melts and hardens creating a robust, water-tight and often slightly translucent body. Stoneware began to be produced in China in the Shang dynasty (1700–1027BC) and by the Han dynasty (206BC–220AD) had become refined enough to be considered more than just a utilitarian material. A range of small objects for the educated élite, such as water-droppers (used in calligraphy), oil lamps and vases, began to be made, often in the form of animals like frogs and rams. These pieces were often decorated using a roulette wheel with incised or carved repeating patterns.

Celadon, the most famous type of Chinese stoneware, was produced in two main centres. A distinctive olive-green coloured celadon was produced in the north-west region of China in Henan and Shaanxi during the Song dynasty (960–1279). After this time the southern celadons of Longquan (in Zhejiang) became the main centres of production and wares were made in a soft blue-green colour.

Among the other important types of stoneware made in China was Cizhou ware, which was produced mainly in the northern provinces of Henan, Hebei and Shaanxi. Pieces are often highly decorative, characteristically adorned with painted, incised or punched designs which proved to be inspirational in the 20th century for modern studio potters such as Bernard Leach (see p152). Jun wares are another highly sought-after type of Chinese stoneware. Produced in Linru, central Henan, these pieces were typically heavily potted and thickly glazed in various shades of blue, sometimes with splashes of purple and, more rarely, celadon-like green.

Although larger examples of Chinese stoneware are keenly collected and often attract very high prices, small, less rare items such as teabowls are readily available for modest sums and can form an interesting and visually appealing collection.

◀ **YUE WARE**
This oval jar dates from 265–317AD and was probably inspired by metal vessels. It is typically glazed in an olive-green colour; often (as pictured here) the glaze does not cover the entire outer surface and where the base has been left exposed the body has fired to a reddish colour in the kiln.
$2,250–3,750

▶ **NORTHERN CELADON**
Bowls are the most commonly seen examples of northern Chinese celadon, and this one (12thC) is of typical conical form with an olive-green glaze and moulded floral decoration. If the decoration is carved or includes figures the value increases.
$2,250–3,000

◀ JUN WARE

This small shallow dish (12th–13thC) is one of the most common Jun shapes. Pieces such as this were fairly robustly potted, with a thick wedge-shaped footrim measuring about ¼in (0.5cm) across. Colours range from this pale lavender glaze, to a greener blue and dark blue and purple. The glaze was generously applied and dribbles on the underside are also typical of this type of ware. $2,250–3,000

▶ BLACKWARE TEABOWLS

This late Song teabowl made in the Fujian province has a typical form with a shallow ridge beneath the rim so it could be easily held. Bowls like this were first used in monasteries by Buddhist monks who introduced tea drinking to China. Glazes on blackware vary from black to this streaked dark brown glaze known as "hare's fur". $2,250–3,000

◀ STEM BOWLS

Stem bowls were used for ritual purposes and the earliest date from the Tang dynasty. This 15th-century Longquan example is typically coated in a thick glaze that softens the contours of the body, although around the rim you can just see the white body where the glaze has run during firing. $2,250–3,000

BEWARE

Celadon has long been coveted by collectors and has never really been out of production. Modern imitations of southern celadon pieces are in most respects, apart from their slightly mechanical and glassy appearance, very similar to the originals.

CHINESE PORCELAIN

Porcelain evolved gradually from the high-fired white wares made in China in the Tang dynasty (c.618–906), the earliest pieces were greyish or creamy and slightly gritty in appearance. By the Song dynasty (960–1279) forms were increasingly sophisticated, their shapes and decoration often inspired by flowers such as the lotus, chrysanthemum and peony. In the northern region of Dingyao potters began producing carved and moulded porcelain bowls and dishes, fired in coal kilns producing an ivory or buff-coloured appearance. Underglaze blue decoration on porcelain first began to be used c.1330 and most early wares were decorated in bands or registers of pattern. The overall effect is crowded and complex by comparison with the more balanced and spacious designs of early Ming. By the 15th century the first polychrome wares began to be produced although some of these later wares are not as skilfully painted as the renowned *doucai* porcelain of the Chenghua period (1465–87). Ding ware remains rare and expensive; imperial Ming porcelain is among the most valuable of all early Chinese ceramics. By contrast in southern Qingbai huge quantities of bluish and greenish bowls survive and these are still modestly priced.

◀ DINGYAO
The warm ivory tone and moulded floral decoration are characteristic of Dingyao. This porcellaneous stoneware dish dates from 1115–1234 and was glazed and fired upside down hence the metal-bound rim to protect the unglazed edge. The double gourd ewer characterizes the elegance of northern Song and was made 960–1127.
Dish $4,500–7,500;
ewer $6,000–9,000

MARKS
Marks first became used regularly during the Ming dynasty in the reign of Xuande c.1426 and usually comprise four or six characters. By c.1500 marks on Chinese porcelain are usually those of earlier reigns.

德年製　大明宣

▶ CARVED DECORATION
Superior carved decoration increases the value of early Chinese porcelain. This 13th-century Qingbai (Yinqing) ewer for oil or wine is typically thinly potted and made of a chalk-white sugary body covered in a thin semi-translucent bluish glaze. The name Yingqing in fact means shadowy or misty blue.
$1,500–2,250

◀ EARLY YUAN
◀ EARLY YUAN UNDERGLAZE DECORATION

The decoration on early blue and white porcelain was usually divided into separate registers or panels, each of which could be completed by a different hand. The decoration on this Yuan *kendi* (left) and ewer (right) has several registers decorated with classic scrolls, plantain leaves and squared scroll bands. $4,500–7,500 each

▶ MING BLUE AND WHITE

A late Ming blue and white saucer dish of the second half of the 16th century; the traditional twin fish design denotes marital fidelity and harmony. Note that the blue decoration has characteristic flecks which have been caused by oxidization through the glaze. $4,500–7,500

◀ MING POLYCHROME DECORATION

The typical palette of blue, iron red, dirty yellow, green and manganese-brown was created by first painting the design in underglaze blue, firing, enamelling with the other colours and refiring. Although designs such as those used on this *wucai* square dish (1573–1619) are rather confused, they have great charm and are highly sought after by collectors. $3,000–4,500

CHINESE EXPORT

The large-scale export of Chinese ceramics to Europe began shortly after the arrival of the Portuguese in China in 1517. Thousands of pieces went to Lisbon as ballast in ships laden with spices, lacquer, silks and other luxury items. Throughout the 17th century the Dutch monopolized the trade with China and Japan, while the English dominated the export of porcelain throughout the 18th century. Early export goods are sometimes indistinguishable from those made for the home market, and it was not until the 17th century that the Dutch began requesting European shapes such as mustard pots, cuspidors (spittoons), coffee pots and narrow-necked jugs. By the 18th century there was also a thriving demand for armorial porcelain. The trade in Chinese export porcelain waned as European porcelain factories and creamware became increasingly competitive in the late 1700s. After 1735, instead of potting and enamelling wares in the potteries and shipping them to Canton (Guangzhou) for export, porcelain was dispatched from the potteries in the white (when it was less fragile) and enamelling shops were set up in the Canton area; vast quantities of decorative "Canton" wares were made throughout the 19th and 20th centuries.

Much export porcelain is still readily available at modest sums and you can find pairs of polychrome or blue and white plates for between $400 and $600.

▶ **KRAAK-PORSELEIN**

The early export wares made in the Ming period were often decorated with panels filled with repeating flowers, animals, birds or figures and this distinctive type of decoration is known as *kraak-porselein*. (*Kraak* is a Dutch word for the type of Portuguese ship that transported this sort of porcelain.) This bottle is a good example of the characteristic simple style. $1,500–2,250

◀ **FAMILLE VERTE**
Another popular palette for export wares was formed of translucent colours known as *famille verte* ("green family"); this replaced the old *wucai* palette and used overglaze blue and slightly raised enamelling. The decorative figure in a garden was a favourite theme in the Qing dynasty. $600–900

► **SHAPES**

The influence of French silver designs is reflected in this mid–18th-century hexagonal dish. The decoration is fairly dense and detailed and the blue underglaze decoration is very pure – later it became greyer and the decoration was less accomplished. $300–375

MARKS

Marks on Chinese export porcelain include:
• symbols such as a tripod, lozenges, lotus and artemisia leaf
• earlier reign marks.

▼ **CANTON** *FAMILLE ROSE*

Canton porcelain of the 19th century is usually crammed with figures and detail, and pink, turquoise and gilding are predominant. This large vase is typically colourful. $1,800–2,400

▲ *FAMILLE ROSE*

From c.1718 onwards porcelain in the *famille rose* palette was decorated using colours to which white had been added to make them opaque. Despite the slightly misleading term *famille rose* (meaning "pink family"), pink is not necessarily the dominant shade. The scattered decoration of this 18th-century dish is typical of the export ware of that period. $150–300

KOREAN CERAMICS

Among the earliest Korean ceramics to survive are unglazed stonewares produced from about 100AD. These were simply decorated with repeating motifs incised or punched into the surface. Celadon stonewares reflecting the influence of Chinese pottery rank among Korean potters' most beautiful achievements, and enjoyed a golden age from 1150–1250. Another important type of stoneware, Punch'ong ware, was similar to celadon but more elaborately decorated with stamped designs decorated with white slip (see p62). Porcelain was produced by Korean potters from the 11th century onwards, but although Korean porcelain often reflects the inspiration of Chinese design, it is usually identifiable by its idiosyncratic imperfections. Unfortunately, the paste tended to sag during firing and you will frequently find pieces of irregular shape or with splits and flaws.

Nevertheless Korean ceramics are highly collectable and even 19th-century examples can attract high prices. Surprisingly, the more affordable collecting areas include very early stonewares, which are often relatively modestly priced considering their age.

◀ KOREAN CELADON
Korean potters were the only manufacturers of early celadon to use inlaid decoration. Designs cut out of the clay body were filled with white or black slips; this 13th century pear-shaped bottle has a white floral and geometric design. Other celadon wares were decorated with moulded, stamped or carved designs. $3,000–6,000

DECORATION
A wide variety of techniques were used on Korean celadon:
- moulding or stamping
- carving
- incising
- inlaying incised designs with coloured slip.

▲ WARES
Porcelain objects for the scholar's table, such as brush droppers, brush holders and censers, were produced in Korea in the 18th and 19th centuries. Some pieces, such as this two-handled censer, are adorned somewhat casually with some sort of pierced decoration, which was very popular in the late Yi dynasty (16th–19thC). $2,250–3,000

▶ **UNDERGLAZE BLUE DECORATION**
This 19th-century blue and white globular bottle with a tall neck is painted with a typical soft greyish underglaze blue design of a coiled dragon. Other favourite motifs include bamboo, peony flowers, birds, landscapes and roundels.
$1,500–2,750

▲ **KOREAN STONEWARES**
This Korean stoneware bowl is decorated in olive-green on a white ground. The slightly angular bulbous shape was popular in the late 15th and 16th centuries, both in Korea and Japan.
$5,000–15,000

IDENTIFICATION
THE UNDERSIDE OF THIS 13TH CENTURY INCISED CELADON LOTUS BOWL HAS MANY OF THE IMPERFECTIONS YOU WILL FIND ON KOREAN CERAMICS.
$2,250–3,000

Pieces are usually slightly irregular in shape.

Glazes often show signs of discoloration.

Firing flaws and other imperfections are typical.

Note the three large, gritty tripod marks on the base – they are often more irregular than this.

The soft paste often split during firing.

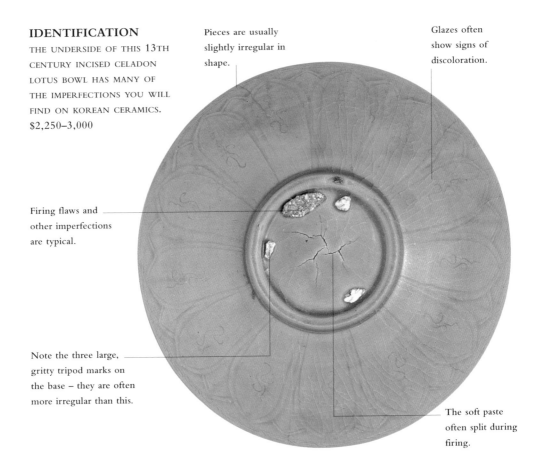

EARLY JAPANESE CERAMICS

Stoneware has been produced in Japan from Neolithic times but unlike their Chinese counterparts the Japanese did not begin producing porcelain until the early 17th century. Many Japanese ceramics reflect the cross-fertilization of ideas from China mingled with distinctively Japanese elements. Stonewares show the influence of blackware and celadon in characteristic regional styles. Early porcelain wares were made in white or blue and white, and by 1650 the Japanese had established a market in export wares with Dutch traders. Kakiemon and Imari, the two most famous types of Japanese coloured enamel decoration, were developed in the second half of the century. After the civil wars in China (c.1680) the Chinese began to produce much less expensive porcelain than the Japanese. By 1757 the Dutch had virtually ceased trading porcelain with Japan. The Japanese export market dwindled until its revival in the late 19th century. The vast majority of Japanese ceramics made for Western markets therefore predate c.1760 or were made after c.1860.

> **MARKS**
> With a few exceptions, the only marks on Japanese porcelain are borrowed from the Chinese reign marks of the Ming dynasty.

▶ **ARITA PORCELAIN**

Arita porcelain takes its name from the region of northern Kyushu, Japan where many kilns were centred. Vast quantities of blue and white wares, such as this *Enghalskrug* or narrow-necked jug, were produced for the export market. This example dates from c.1660–80 and was probably intended to be metal-mounted. $3,000–4,500

◀ **DECORATION**
Designs on late 17th- and early 18th-century porcelain are often stiffly painted because the decorators worked from crudely copied wooden patterns given to them by the Dutch. The shape of this *kendi* (c.1665) is also based on Chinese forms; although intended originally to hold purified water, export *kendi* were often used as hookah bases. $2,250–3,000

◀ KAKIEMON
Named after a celebrated potter, Kakiemon porcelain is recognizable by its distinctive palette and often sparse decoration. Colours used include iron red, deep sky blue, turquoise, yellow, aubergine/manganese and black. Decoration is delicate and allows much of the white porcelain to show. The floral pattern on this lobed dish (c.1700) is asymmetrical – another typical Kakiemon feature. $4,500–7,500

▼ VASES
Vases like this (early 18thC) were popular export items and have a distinctive shape with straight conical sides on a ridged foot and a deep cover with flanges that protrude at a sharp angle. Covers may have finials in the shape of a tall flame, an animal or a figure. Most were originally from a garniture which included three vases and matching tall beakers that would have been displayed on chimneypieces or cabinets. $9,000–12,000

▲ IMARI
Elaborately decorated wares in a characteristic palette of blue, iron red and gilding are classified as Imari wares – the name comes from the port where such pieces were shipped. Imari porcelain may also include shades of greenish yellow, turquoise and manganese. This large dish (c.1700) is typically decorated with an elaborate design known as "three friends", showing figures among rock work. $4,500–7,500

LATER JAPANESE CERAMICS

The Japanese ceramics industry enjoyed a revival of popularity in the late 19th century when trading links with the Western world were reestablished. Most 19th-century ceramics repeat earlier styles often with complex shapes. As production increased, underglaze blue was often applied by stencil and decoration appears stiff by comparison with earlier wares. Satsuma stonewares enjoyed a heyday of popularity in the late 19th and early 20th centuries, and these highly decorative pieces decorated with a crackled creamy glaze, heavy gilding and subdued colours are widely available. Prices depend mainly on size and visual appeal of the decoration. From c.1900, another prolific and successful manufacturer of porcelain aimed at the European market was Noritake. This factory is still in production today but early pieces reflecting the influence of Art Nouveau and Art Deco are becoming increasingly sought after, and there is a specialist club for Noritake collectors.

◀ SATSUMA
This high-shouldered jar decorated with women and children gathering blossom has many features that are typical of 19th-century Satsuma stoneware including: a creamy wash ground; elaborate figurative subject – geisha or holy men are also favourite subjects; lavish gilding overlaid with a geometrical floral design. By this time many better-quality pieces of pottery were signed, as this is. A signature may add slightly to value. $3,750–5,250

▶ FUKAGAWA
Naturalism is a dominant theme in later decoration and although this heavy baluster jar is painted in traditional colours with a favourite theme – carp among a fishing net – the sense of movement is typical of the better-quality wares of the late 19th century. $1,500–2,250

MATERIALS
- Earthenwares produced for the home and export markets: Satsuma, Kyoto, Awara
- Porcelain for home and export: Arita, Imari, Fukagawa, Hirado, Seto, Noritake.

▶ STYLE

The decoration on later Imari porcelain, such as this large charger (c.1880) tends to be very dense. The colour balance changes subtly so that red rather than blue is generally the dominant shade. The vessel in front is a traditional 17th-century form, based on a wooden pail. Dish $900–1,500; charger $750–1,050

▼ VALUE

Later Japanese ceramics vary enormously in quality. These Satsuma censers (c.1900–10) are crowded with scenes of holy men painted predominantly in shades of gold and russet. Pieces such as this were exported in vast quantity to the West as decorative items rather than refined works of art. $600–750

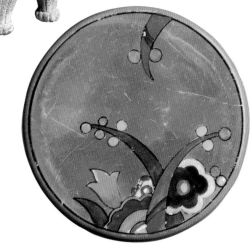

MARKS
- Imari is unmarked or occasionally has an impressed stamp.
- Noritake has a fleur-de-lis motif.
- Good Kyoto and Satsuma often carry the potter's name.
- Fukagawa has a Mount Fuji mark.

▶ NORITAKE

In the early 20th century Noritake produced hand-painted wares at a price comparable to printed European ceramics. This plate, with its stylized floral decoration, reflects the influence of Art Deco. Noritake exported large quantities of wares to America. Many of its 1920s and 1930s designs were conceived in America by eminent designers such as Frank Lloyd Wright. $60–90

Richly diverse Islamic pottery has throughout the centuries exerted a powerful influence over the development of ceramics in the West. The Islamic world spanned from Spain in the West, to the Indus valley in the East and this vast area was responsible for a similarly huge range of decorative traditions and potting techniques.

The first main centres of pottery production included Mesopotamia, the fertile plain between the rivers Tigris and Euphrates, where tin-glazed earthenware and lustre decoration were developed and refined between the 8th and 13th centuries. From the Middle Ages until the 15th century Persian centres in Kashan and Rayy (in what is now Iran) were preeminent, producing elaborately decorated lustre pottery decorated with intricate calligraphic designs or naturalistic patterns. In the 16th and 17th centuries the southern and eastern areas of Persia rose to prominence producing blue and white wares intended to rival Chinese porcelain, and were sometimes even sold to unwary buyers as the genuine article.

Among the most famous examples of Islamic pottery are wares made by Turkish potters around Iznik and later at Kutahya. These colourful pieces were made from the 15th century onwards and their distinctive patterns include many of the flowers that grew wild in the surrounding area such as tulips and carnations. Turkish potters produced a wide range of wares including tiles for mosques and other buildings as well as objects such as candlesticks and lamps, and tablewares including such items as bowls, plates and cups.

ISLAMIC POTTERY

Few pieces of Islamic pottery are marked and attributions are reliant on knowledge of the decoration and pottery bodies produced in each area. Although Islamic pottery is internationally collected, the field is particularly popular with Middle Eastern buyers. With European collectors, Iznik pottery is among the most popular of all types of Islamic ceramics and public interest has been boosted by recent research. Early wares fetch relatively high prices, but later pieces decorated with traditional patterns are available for modest sums.

▲ **LUSTREWARES** This elegant pear-shaped 17th-century bottle, probably made in Kashan, is an example of lustre decoration. The technique involved decorating the pottery with metal oxides such as gold and silver and firing the piece in a reducing atmosphere so that the oxygen is taken from the compound to leave pure metal behind. $3,000–4,500

▶ **PERSIAN BLUE & WHITE**
Some of the finest Middle Eastern blue and white pottery, such as this 17th-century *kendi*, was produced in Meshed and Kirman in eastern and southern Persia and designs rely heavily on those of Chinese late Ming and transitional porcelain. Unlike Chinese porcelain, some Persian examples are outlined in black. $2,250–3,000

▲ **TILES**
Iznik potters produced large numbers of tiles and this is a fine example, typically brilliantly coloured with bright cobalt, turquoise and Armenian bole (red). The tulip and carnation motifs are among the most popular of all on Iznik pottery. $1,200–1,800

▶ **PERSIAN FRITWARE**
A fine example of turquoise glazed fritware, this elegant vase was probably produced in Persia in the 13th or 14th century. Fritware was made from a silica-rich clay which when fired formed a semi-translucent body with a glassy appearance. $1,800–2,700

◀ **IZNIK DESIGNS**
Many Iznik designs were loosely derived from Chinese porcelain. Both the lotus (left) and the whorl (right) designs are from early Ming (16thC–17thC) border patterns.
Left $1,200–1,800; right $1,050–1,500

Pottery had been made in Europe from Neolithic times but the Arab invasion of Spain in the 8th century marked an important turning point in its evolution. The Moors introduced lustre and other sophisticated glazes, which had been evolved in Egypt and Mesopotamia. These new techniques enabled potters to make objects of unrivalled sophistication and pieces of pottery achieved the status of decorative works of art rather than being merely regarded as utilitarian objects.

Gradually during the centuries that followed, potters in Italy, France, Germany and Holland evolved their own distinctive decorative styles and potting techniques. The earliest European pottery that collectors are likely to see is made from an earthenware body which has been lead-glazed to make it watertight. One of the largest pottery "families" was tin-glazed earthenware. Known as maiolica in Italy, faience in France, Delft in the Netherlands and delftware in England, tin glaze was so opaque that it allowed potters to simulate the effect of white porcelain. Other early wares include stoneware discovered by potters in the Rhineland who also developed salt glazes. As more refined bodies such as creamware were developed in the 18th century, and new glazing techniques evolved, so too did new styles of decoration. The patterns with which pottery is adorned reflect the prevailing fashion for Baroque, Rococo and Classical ornament.

For collectors European pottery offers a hugely diverse and fascinating collecting area at a similarly varied range of prices.

SPAIN & PORTUGAL

Spain is especially noted for its fine lustrewares that were made from at least the 14th century onwards in the centres of Málaga and Manises. Production of Spanish lustre continued until the 18th century and beyond but the finest and most valuable pieces are those of the 14th and 15th centuries. Early wares are dominated by Islamic motifs; later on, European designs prevail. Other leading Spanish pottery centres where polychrome wares were produced include Talavera de la Reina, Puente del Arzobispo, and later Alcora. In the 19th century primitively decorated earthenware replaced the sophisticated pottery of earlier times. Early examples of Spanish pottery are rare and fetch extremely high prices; non-armorial pieces from the 16th and 17th centuries sell for between $1,500 and $3,000; prices for small bowls and dishes from the 17th century begin at around $150.

▲ EARLY DESIGNS
This dish (c.1400) is skilfully painted with a repeated tree of life motif and symbols representing benevolence. The colours, cobalt and lustre, have been applied in two stages. Early pieces of this quality are rare and values high.
$15,000–18,000

◀ PORTUGUESE POTTERY

Loose, flowing brushwork is a characteristic feature of much of 17th-century Portuguese pottery, which was often based on Chinese Ming designs. Here the figure of the deer is derived from Chinese ceramics; it has, however, been westernized by the addition of antlers. $1,500–2,250

MARKS

It is rare to find Spanish pottery that has been marked by its factory; however, some later pieces made in the centres of Talavera de la Reina and Alcora may be found to have factory marks.

▶ LATER LUSTRE

Reproductions of early designs were made in Spain and Italy from the last quarter of the 19th century onwards. The decoration of these blue and copper lustre chargers has a crowded mechanical appearance that points to a date in the late 19th century. $300–450

◀ TALAVERA POTTERY

Inkwells such as this were made in the 17th century at Talavera de la Reina and Puente del Arzobispo in Spain. The crude feathery decoration in cobalt, manganese and ochre is a characteristic feature of these pieces. $225–375

▲ DECORATION

Repeating patterns were much used on Spanish and Portuguese pieces after the 15th century. The spiral moulded border on this early 16th century dish was inspired by silver designs and the intricate knot patterns and geometric designs were very popular. $2,250–3,000

ITALY & SICILY

The technique of making tin-glazed earthenwares called maiolica developed in Italy in the 15th century, in the important centres of Deruta and Gubbio. The earliest pieces were adorned with primitive designs and a limited palette but gradually decoration became increasingly sophisticated – often based on engravings of ornamental subjects or narrative scenes – and an increasingly wide range of colours were used. By the 16th century Castel Durante, Urbino and Siena emerged as lead-ing areas of production and a fully developed style evolved, known as "beautiful style". Shapes became increasingly ambitious and many pieces were based on Mannerist silver forms. In the 17th and 18th centuries high-quality pottery was produced in Venice and Castelli and the influence of Chinese porcelain and an interest in classicism are reflected in many of the subjects chosen for decoration. Pottery was also made in several centres in Sicily, most notably in Palermo.

▶ **LUSTREWARE**
Lustre was probably introduced to Italy from Spain in the late 15th century and Deruta, where this charger (c.1520) was made, emerged as an important pottery centre. The Cupid which decorates the centre was probably copied from a woodblock print and the piece is painted using lustre blue for the outline of the design. $12,000–18,000

▲ **DRUG JARS**
Jars made for storing drugs are divided into two main types: this one has a spout and was meant to hold wet drugs; those of straighter form and with no spout, known as *albarelli* (see right), were for dry drugs. The jar above dates from the late 17th century and is simply decorated in blue and white, in a style typical of Savona where it was made. $1,050–1,500

◀ *ALBARELLI*
Used in pharmacies and hospitals from late medieval times, the *albarello* was derived from Islamic pottery. This one was made in Sicily c.1600 and is decorated with a portrait of a saint surrounded with trophies. Sicilian pottery commands a premium and this is considerably more valuable than Italian *albarelli* of similar date and decoration. $3,000–4,500

▶ **LATER ITALIAN MAIOLICA**

Ulysse Cantagalli was one of the most prolific manufacturers of late 19th-century reproductions. He marked his wares with a cockerel. This Cantagalli two-handled oval bowl painted in the Urbino style with a landscape is typical of late 19th-early 20th-century imitations of earlier Italian maiolica. Even so it would be worth $450–750 for decorative appeal alone.

ISTORIATO DISHES

FROM C.1520 POTTERS IN URBINO BEGAN PRODUCING HIGHLY DECORATIVE DISHES WHICH WERE TREATED LIKE A CANVAS AND ENTIRELY COVERED WITH A NARRATIVE SCENE. THIS DISH DATES FROM C.1550, AND IS WORTH $7,500–10,500, BUT SOME *ISTORIATO* DISHES CAN FETCH MUCH MORE. FACTORS AFFECTING VALUE INCLUDE:
- DATE
- QUALITY OF THE PAINTING
- SIGNATURE
- CONDITION.

MARKS
- Early Italian and Sicilian pottery is only sporadically marked. Later wares are more frequently found to be marked – often with the words "Faenza" and "Made in Italy".
- Marks often refer to the individual potter and the town where he was working.
- Rare marks include: Caffaggiolo, Urbino (Castel Durante), Faenza, Gubbio, Savona.

AUTHENTICITY
Copies of *istoriato* dishes were made in the 19th century (see above) and these can even confuse the experts. This dish from an important collection was sold with a thermoluminescence certificate stating it was fired between 350 and 550 years ago.

SUBJECTS
Most scenes are based on engravings illustrating stories by Ovid; this one shows Meleager and the Calydonian Boar.

COLOURS
The predominant shades of ochre and yellow are typical of early *istoriato* pieces; later in the following decades the palette became brighter and more varied.

FRENCH FAIENCE

Early French faience looks very similar to pottery made in Italy because Italian potters migrated to Rouen and Lyons early in the 16th century, bringing with them their native style. Identifiably French faience was being produced in the leading centre of Nevers by the 17th century and styles show the dual influences of Baroque and Chinese design. As the century waned Rouen superseded Nevers as the most important centre and throughout the 18th century potters moved away from the use of hot, high-fired colours to *petit feu*, a more refined, delicate palette. Other important centres of French pottery at this time

included the towns of Strasbourg, Sceaux, Marseilles and Moustiers. During the 19th century French pottery returned to earlier styles and there were few new developments although French creamware called *faïence fine* was made in response to competition from the English company Wedgwood.

The market for French pottery remains largely dominated by collectors in France. Among the most valuable pieces are large early objects such as cisterns and vases. Pieces made in the 19th century in earlier styles are often highly decorative and available to the collector for modest sums.

◀ ROUEN
The blue and red palette and formally painted style of decoration are typical of pottery that was produced in Rouen during the late Baroque period. This large dish dates from c.1720–30 and the central panel showing a vase of flowers on a table and a deer with rockwork is clearly inspired from designs that were frequently used to decorate earlier Chinese porcelain. $3,000–4,500

▶ FORMS
Silver shapes provided the inspiration for many domestic pieces made at the Rouen factories from around the beginning of the 18th century. This helmet-shaped ewer form was popular in both England and France and the combination of blue and red is inspired by the Japanese Imari palette. $4,500–6,000

► **STRASBOURG**
Milk-white, near-perfect glazes and botanical painting of the highest order are characteristic of Strasbourg pottery made in the 18th century. This detail of a delicately painted plate, dominated by puce shows how refined decoration became with the use of typical *petit feu* colours. Some plates of this type are signed on the back and this can add to their value. $3,000–4,500

▲ **LATER POTTERY**
French pottery of the 17th and 18th centuries enjoyed a revival of popularity towards the end of the 19th century. The present-day value of pieces of faience such as this blue and white Nevers-style vase (c.1880–1900) is based mainly on the size and decorative appeal of the individual item. $1,500–2,250

▼ **MARSEILLES**
Eleven factories flourished in the Marseilles region and one of the most famous was Veuve Perrin, where this dish was made c.1760. Pottery decorators were encouraged to attend drawing academies, and this free, spontaneous style of decoration is typical of much Marseilles pottery. $1,800–2,700

VEUVE PERRIN
Pottery made by the Veuve Perrin factory is marked with the initials "VP".

MARKS
Many pieces of French faience are marked with the initials of the maker or with a cipher which is characteristically painted by hand.

DUTCH DELFT

The technique of making tin-glazed earthenware was brought to the Netherlands at the beginning of the 16th century by immigrant Italian potters. By the mid-17th century, as Dutch Delft pottery flourished, the brewing industry declined, and many potteries were set up in disused breweries. This is why there are potteries with names like The Three Barrels, The Two Ships and The Claw. Around 33 factories flourished in the region around Delft, most producing a wide range of ornamental and everyday objects. Blue and white was the dominant palette and the vast majority of wares were heavily influenced by Chinese porcelain imported in huge quantity to Dutch ports. Although Dutch Delft bears a strong resemblance to English wares of similar date collectors should remember that at present prices for Dutch Delft are usually somewhat lower than for English.

► **TILES & PLAQUES**
The Dutch were prolific makers of tiles and plaques and some factories were solely devoted to their output. Most were painted in blue and white or polychrome, and price depends on the quality of decoration and detail. These early 17th-century examples are attractively delineated with slightly unusual subjects and this increases their value. $300–750 each; later versions $75 or less

▲ **EXOTIC OBJECTS**
Objects inspired by Oriental imports were popular in the late 17th and 18th centuries. This metal-mounted ewer, in the style of Chinese export porcelain from the start of the 18th century, shows how Dutch potters responded to the fashion for chinoiserie in their own designs. $2,250–3,750

ENGLISH OR DUTCH?
The following points can help with identification:

Dutch	English
● Ambitious forms	● Simpler forms
● Pinholes in greyish body	● Fine body
● Ambitious brush work	● Simple painted decoration work
● Often marked	● Rarely marked

◀ COWS
Another favourite of Delft potters, cows were made in considerable numbers, usually in white, but sometimes, as in this case, painted. This piece dates from the middle of the 18th century and was probably made to mark an agricultural festival. $1,500–3,000

▶ CONDITION
As with all ceramics condition can have an enormous bearing on price. Because tin-glaze earthenware is a fairly soft material some chipping is to be expected but it is often possible to buy pieces with more serious imperfections at greatly reduced prices. This plate, however, is by the most sought-after of all Dutch pottery painters, Frederich van Frytom, so the value remains extremely high. $15,000–22,500

BEWARE
Later copies of earlier, more valuable styles often carry the phoney marks of famous factories such as APK and PAK, and these marks should therefore not be relied upon for identification.

◀ GARNITURES
Inspired by Chinese porcelain versions that were imported into the country, the Dutch Delft potters first produced garnitures in the 17th century. This 19th-century vase is part of a five-piece garniture in the Cachemire style made originally in the early 18th century. The sides are ribbed and decorated with elaborate panels of flowers. Even though it is a later copy it is highly decorative and the set would still be worth $6,000–10,500.

GERMANY

Stonewares were made in the Sieburg and Cologne areas of the Rhineland from the late Middle Ages and evolved independently of those made in China. Regional specialities became gradually more pronounced and by the 17th century Westerwald, Cologne, Frechen, Raeren and Kreussen were all important centres of stoneware production.

German potters also made faience and the industry was well established by the second half of the 17th century in Frankfurt, Hanau and later Berlin. German faience is easily confused with Dutch Delft and heavily influenced by Chinese designs. Early wares were mainly confined to bulbous jugs known as *Birnkrug* and *Enghalskrug*, and deep dishes known as *Buckelplatte,* while in the 18th century cylindrical tankards called *Walzenkrug* were made. These usually have hinged pewter lids and footrims and are available for modest sums.

◀ WESTERWALD

This stoneware *Kugelbauchkrug,* or fat-bellied tankard, was made in the Westerwald region c.1710 for the English market. It is decorated with a portrait of Queen Anne and has several features typical of Westerwald pottery: moulded and applied, and incised motifs; a blue wash ground; detailing in manganese. Similar jugs with portraits of George I are more common and therefore less valuable. $750–1,200

▶ BELLARMINES

These bulbous jugs, named after Cardinal Roberto Bellarmino, were produced in Cologne and Frechen, where this one was made in the 17th century. The brown mottled glaze, known as "tiger skin", is a characteristic feature of these jugs. $750–1,050

BEWARE

The base of genuine bellarmines should have an impressed oval mark like a thumb print where the piece was removed from the wheel. Later copies are flat on the base.

▲ TANKARDS

Faience tankards were produced in large quantities in Germany throughout the 18th century and this particular example is decorated with a favourite German motif – a bird among sponged foliage. Tankards are sometimes marked on the base but most are not. $1,500–2,700

▶ **FRANKFURT**

The blue and white figures in landscapes which decorate these Frankfurt faience bottles (made c.1700) are based on Chinese designs in the "transitional" style, one of the most important influences on European pottery in the latter 17th century. The brilliant shade of blue is a sign of quality and adds to their decorative appeal.
$1,500–3,000 (for the pair)

▲ **STYLES & DECORATION**

Spirally moulded forms, derived from silver shapes, were produced in the southern regions of Frankfurt, Hanau, Ansbach and Nuremberg; the scattered floral decoration is typical of Frankfurt faience made c.1700. $3,000–4,500

▼ **WIESBADEN**

One of several minor producers of German faience in the late 18th century, the Wiesbaden factory specialized in scattered floral decoration painted in green, a form of decoration known as *en camaïeu vert*. This bullet-shaped teapot (c.1775) is slightly damaged, hence the relatively low value. Pieces are sometimes marked on the base, as this one is, "WD".
$900–1,350

British Pottery

Most collectable British pottery dates from c.1650 onwards; earlier pieces are scarce and usually highly priced. Throughout the 17th and early 18th centuries lead-glazed wares dominated production and today their naive charm and colourful decorative appeal make them highly sought after by collectors. As the 18th century progressed new materials and glazes evolved and certain makers, such as Whieldon and Wedgwood, became associated with certain types of ware. English pottery is therefore categorized in a variety of ways: by the type of body (creamware, basalt, agateware, redware); its glaze or decoration (salt glaze, lead glaze, lustre); or by the name of the potter with whom it is associated (Whieldon ware, Prattware).

The production of all ceramics depends on the ready availability of the necessary raw materials and for this reason the Staffordshire region, where there were rich deposits of clay and readily available fuel, dominated pottery production from the late 18th century onwards. Among the potters who flourished in the region were Whieldon, Spode and Wedgwood.

Potteries became increasingly mechanized during the 19th and 20th century; output increased and these pieces are available for modest sums today. In the late 19th century the reaction against industrialization inspired a revival of hand-crafted pottery, and studio potteries such as the Martin Brothers and William de Morgan flourished. In the 20th century modern designs became an important element in industrial pottery. Today designs by Clarice Cliff, Eric Ravilious and Keith Murray are highly sought after.

ENGLISH DELFTWARE

Rather confusingly tinglaze earthenware made in England is known as "English delftware", while tin glaze made in the Netherlands is called "Delftware". London was the most important early centre of English delftware and after c.1650 centres were established in Bristol, Brislington, Liverpool, Glasgow and Dublin. English delftware is characterized by its simple forms and colourful decoration, much of which shows the influence of Chinese porcelain. Among the most sought-after pieces are the "blue dash chargers": large dishes so called because of the blue strokes that decorate the rims. Rare examples can fetch tens of thousands of pounds although damaged pieces are far less valuable. Unlike most ceramics, prices for early delft are hardly affected by damage, as pieces are so scarce.

▲ COMMEMORATIVE CHARGERS
Chargers decorated with portraits of monarchs, popular members of the royal family or military leaders feature Charles I and II, William and Mary, Queen Anne and George I, II and III. Value depends on rarity and on the complexity of the background. The sponged trees seen on this Bristol example with a portrait of William and Mary (c.1690) are among the simplest of backgrounds to be found on chargers. $3,750–5,250

◀ **SUBJECT MATTER**
Among the most sought-after delftware subjects are the "farmyard" series – plates decorated with various birds and domestic animals, including peacocks, cockerels and hounds, or as here an egret with a worm in its beak. Blue and white is less valuable than polychrome so this plate (c.1920–40) is worth $3,000–3,750.

MARKS
Although often dated, English delftware is not usually marked and can therefore be confused with Dutch Delft which is usually less valuable (see p56 for differences).

▲ **DECORATION**
Painted decoration tended to become increasingly sensitive and sophisticated as the 18th century progressed. The delicately painted landscape with figures that decorated this vase are typical of the mid-18th century and similar decoration is also seen on plates, dishes and other wares. $2,250–3,000

▲ **POSSET JUGS**
Posset jugs like this were used for a slightly alcoholic gruel or porridge which was drunk from the spout, and were made from the mid-17th century to the mid-18th century. The bulbous form with two handles and curving spout is the most commonly seen. $2,250–3,750

WHAT TO LOOK FOR
Among other forms of unusual and decorative English delftware, you can find the following:
- shaving and bleeding bowls
- puzzle jugs
- flower bricks
- shoes
- apothecaries' pill slabs.

SLIPWARE

Slipware is so called because the earthenware body was decorated with "slip": a creamy solution of different coloured clays and water. Pieces were usually dipped into white slip and then extra details were applied by trailing, dotting and combing other slips of varying russet and chocolate colours onto the surface of the body. Decorated pieces were then coated in a thick lead glaze that turned the white clay yellow when the piece was fired.

The overall effect has a primitive charm that collectors in Britain and the United States seem to find highly appealing. Early slipware, which was made from the beginning of the 17th century in Staffordshire and elsewhere in England, can fetch extremely high prices.

▶ **MAKERS**
Rare early pieces marked with the name of their makers are generally the most sought-after slipwares. This armorial charger (c.1685) is marked by William Talor. Other names to keep a lookout for include: Thomas Toft, George Talor, John Wright, John Simpson and Samuel Malkin.
$30,000–45,000

◀ **DECORATION**
This handsome large circular dish (c.1690–1710) is based on silver shapes from Holland and Germany. The simple decoration was created by dipping the piece into cream slip and then trailing and dotting the dark brown, chestnut and cream slip to form this particularly striking decorative effect.
$6,000–7,500

▶ **VALUE**
Makers of slipware did not generally mark their pieces; most names or initials refer to the owner rather than the maker. Because this posset cup, made c.1690, has been inscribed with the name of its original owner, the value is enormously boosted. Even though the piece has fairly serious damage it would still be worth $7,500–12,000

OWL JUGS

AMONG THE MOST DECORATIVE AND VALUABLE PIECES OF SLIPWARE, OWL JUGS SUCH AS THIS ONE (MADE C.1700) WERE MOST PROBABLY USED FOR DRINKING TOASTS TO WELCOME GUESTS. JUGS LIKE THIS HAVE BEEN WIDELY FAKED BUT THIS PARTICULAR EXAMPLE HAS MANY OF THE SIGNS OF AUTHENTICITY YOU SHOULD LOOK FOR ON A GENUINE PIECE.
$22,500–30,000

The glaze is beginning to break and crackle.

There are signs of wear on the studs.

The handle is irregularly shaped and heavy – a fake would probably be more even and finer.

This marbled effect, a favourite technique with slipware potters, was created by dipping the piece into brown and cream slip and then combing the two to mix them slightly.

The base is also thickly potted and uneven – again, fakes tend to be thinner and rather regular in finish.

LATER SLIPWARES

Slipware continued to be made in Britain throughout the 19th century. Affordably priced baking dishes and other utilitarian wares invariably have great charm and can form a highly decorative collection.

▶ WARES

Slipware was also popular for humble domestic wares such as this late 17th-century baluster mug. The robust form is typical of the less elaborate pieces of the time but the date adds value. Such pieces were made to be used and may be damaged – this is slightly cracked and chipped. $7,500–10,500

SALT-GLAZED STONEWARE

Salt-glazed stoneware is made by firing pottery in the kiln to a high temperature (2,500°F (1,400°C)) and then throwing in salt. Sodium from the salt combines with silicates in the clay to form a glassy glaze with a distinctive granular surface – often described as looking like the skin of an orange. The technique was developed in Germany and spread to England in the late 17th century, when it was patented by John Dwight of Fulham, London. Throughout the 18th century salt-glazed wares were made in large quantities in Staffordshire and Nottinghamshire. Teawares and tablewares were the commonest products but various decorative items were also made, including pew groups, cats and other animals. Later pieces were sometimes decorated with transfer prints. Early sculptural pieces tend to attract extremely high prices but you can find moulded plates and other smaller objects from $150. Among the more unusual forms of stoneware is agateware, in which differently coloured clays were rolled together to produce an attractive marbled effect. Popular in the 18th century, agateware was often astonishingly sharply cast and forms often reflect the shapes of silver of the same date. Pieces such as pecten shell teapots and caddies can fetch $1,500.

► DECORATION
Most salt glaze was finished with moulded decoration and then covered in a cream-coloured glaze. Pieces decorated with coloured enamels such as this green teapot decorated with large pink roses (c.1760) are much less common and therefore highly collectable. Other typically coloured grounds include blue and aubergine. $3,000–6,000

◄ RARITY
Although made in the 18th century at a similar date to the teapot above, this example is rather more ambitious in form and the raised moulded cartouche or decorative frame around the painted scene is a rare feature. The pink ground colour is also unusual. $6,000–9,000

▶ **LOVING CUPS**
Two-handled loving cups originally symbolized friendship and trust; later on they became associated with christenings and weddings. It is also possible to find three-handled cups and these are known as "tygs". This typical mid-18th century example is of the two-handled variety and is inscribed with its original owner's initials and is dated 1756. $3,000–4,500

◀ **NOTTINGHAM STONEWARE**
Brown stoneware was a speciality of potters in the Nottingham region during the 18th century. This pierced tankard has a double shell so it still holds liquid. $2,250–3,000

▶ **SGRAFFITO DECORATION**
Incised or scratched decoration, known as sgraffito, was used on stoneware from the third quarter of the 18th century. Simple foliate subjects and inscriptions typically painted in blue, as seen on this small tea caddy, are characteristic. $3,000–4,500

▲ **STYLES**
The influence of contemporary silver design can be seen in the form of this candlestick (c.1750); the heavily scrolled, foliate base reflects the Rococo style and the form of the piece is more ambitious than most. $1,500–2,250

WHIELDON & OTHER COLOURED LEAD-GLAZED WARES

Thomas Whieldon, one of the most famous of the early Staffordshire potters, has given his name to a type of ware decorated with distinctive mottled glazes. The effect was created using coloured lead glazes which mingled together during firing. Whieldon was probably the first potter to develop the coloured lead-glaze technique but numerous other potters in the region also made similar objects; since wares of this type are not generally marked, they are usually called "Whieldon-type". A large proportion of Whieldon ware consists of domestic items such as plates and tewares, or decorative objects such as figurative groups and animals; large hollow wares such as coffee pots are far rarer and therefore tend to command the highest prices. Plates and small jugs will cost under $1,500.

◀ DECORATION
This Whieldon-type cornucopia is typically decorated with applied moulded decoration. Cornucopias (the word means "horn of plenty") were made to attach to a wall and used to hold flowers. You also find salt-glaze versions and both types are highly sought after. $3,750–5,250

WHAT TO LOOK FOR
Several characteristic features can help the collector identify Whieldon ware:
● irregular glaze
● blurred colours that typically run together
● limited palette
● thinly potted body
● slightly iridescent surface covered with regular craquelure, a fine network of cracks running through the glaze.

▲ FRUIT AND VEGETABLES
Naturalistic moulds of cauliflowers, cabbages, lettuces, melons and, as here, pineapples were used by all the Staffordshire potters from the mid-18th century for teapots, coffee pots, tureens and various other objects; this one dates from c.1760. The Victorians later made copies of many of these shapes but they tend to be much more heavily potted and larger, and are far less desirable. $6,000–9,000

▶ **COLOURS**
The coloured glazes used for Whieldon ware are restricted to brown, green, grey, yellow and blue. In this case the plate (c.1760) is glazed in brown and green creating a distinctive blotchy "tortoiseshell" effect. $300–450

TOBY JUGS

AMONG THE AMUSING NOVELTY OBJECTS PRODUCED AFTER C.1750 IN THE STAFFORDSHIRE REGION USING COLOURED LEAD GLAZES ARE TOBY JUGS. THESE RESEMBLE A COMICAL MAN WEARING A TRICORN HAT AND WERE BASED ON HARRY ELWES, A WELL-KNOWN CHARACTER NICKNAMED TOBY PHILPOT BECAUSE OF HIS LEGENDARY CAPACITY FOR DRINK.

Toby jugs originally had a cover in the hat. Most are now missing, but an original cover can considerably increase the value of the piece.

Many different forms of toby jug were made and each is known by a special name; this is the most commonly seen "traditional" type. Other forms of the period include: the Thin Man, the Collier, the Sharp Face, Rodney's Sailor, Admiral Lord Howe, the Coachman, the Fiddler and the Stepped. $2,250–3,000

This is one of the most sought-after toby jugs – made by Ralph Wood II, the colours are well controlled and they have not drifted.

LATER TOBY JUGS
During the late 18th and early 19th centuries brightly coloured Prattware toby jugs were made (see p72) – these are usually worth under $750. Numerous poor-quality copies were also produced in France and elsewhere; these are available for $150 or less.

CREAMWARE & PEARLWARE

During the 1740s a new cream-coloured earthenware with a transparent lead glaze began to make its appearance. Known as creamware, this pottery was refined enough to be considered a substitute for porcelain and from the mid-century was being produced by numerous potters in Staffordshire, Leeds, Liverpool, Bristol and Swansea. Creamware was decorated with moulded decoration, painted enamels or transfer prints and its most successful manufacturer was Josiah Wedgwood

who, as a clever marketing ploy, christened his products "Queensware", ostensibly in deference to Queen Charlotte. Pearlware was a variation of creamware with a slightly blue tinge. Developed by Wedgwood in 1779 it remained popular with several manufacturers throughout much of the 19th century. A huge range of highly decorative objects was made in creamware and pearlware and these remain widely available for modest sums, although early rarities can fetch over $1,500.

▶ **PATTERNS**
Chintz patterns, as used to decorate this globular teapot, were popular decoration for creamwares made c.1770; other popular hand-painted designs include bouquets of flowers, ruined castles and picturesque cottages. $2,250–3,000

▲ **TERMINOLOGY**
There is an overlap between pearlware and Prattware (see p72). Pearlware figures in high-fired colours are often called Prattware. This figure dates from c.1820. $1,800–2,700

▶ **COMMEMORATIVES**
Creamware and pearlware decorated with transfer prints or decorated in low relief with political personalities of the day were popular from the late 18th to mid-19th century. Value depends largely on the rarity of the subject. This particular example of a commemorative plate depicts Admiral Earl Howe and dates from c.1795; it would be worth $750–1,050.

◀ **BOTANICAL SUBJECTS**
Botanical subjects enjoyed a
heyday of popularity during the
early 19th century; this service
dates from c.1810. Most plant
and flower specimens were
copied from contemporary
prints, and pieces such as
these were made in both
England and Wales.
$4,500–6,000 for the set

▶ **SERVICES**
Vast transfer-printed services
were produced in creamware
by Wedgwood and other
manufacturers. Compared with
modern-day equivalents these
can offer surprisingly good
value. This extensive Wedgwood
service (c.1830), transfer-printed
in brown in the Indian Temple
pattern, contains 93 dinner
plates, 20 dessert plates, 23 soup
plates and numerous serving
dishes. $6,700–9,750

◀ **PEARLWARE**
Pearlware was used to produce a
huge variety of decorative figures
and novelty wares, and was left
in the white or decorated with
coloured enamels. Late 18th or
early 19th century models of
sheep like these were a particular
favourite, as were figurative
groups. $1,800–2,750 for a pair

WEDGWOOD

Josiah Wedgwood occupies a pivotal position in the development of ceramics. His factories at Burslem and Etruria were the first to introduce industrial production techniques to pottery. Wedgwood's name is synonymous with several different types of body such as black basalt, *rosso antico*, caneware, jasper ware, agate ware and creamware (see p68), all of which became hugely fashionable and were much copied. A master self-publicist, Wedgwood made high-quality wares that achieved renown throughout England, Europe and America and his fame has endured two centuries. The factory's 20th-century products are of similarly high quality and remain keenly sought after by collectors today (see p146). Wedgwood was also the first potter to commission leading artists to create designs for his products. John Flaxman was responsible for many of the jasper ware designs of the 18th and 19th centuries. The range of Wedgwood available is so enormous that many collectors tend to concentrate on particular objects, on specific types of body or on certain designers. Early marked pieces tend to attract the highest prices.

◀ BLACK BASALT WARE
Basalt ware is among Wedgwood's most popular products, and was produced at the Etruria factory which specialized in ornamental wares. Wedgwood produced a range of library busts of both classical and contemporary figures. This portrait of Sir Walter Scott dates from the 1820s and is quite small (7–8in [18–20cm] high). Some busts are of much larger proportions and were made to stand on top of library bookcases. $300–600

BEWARE
Later in the 19th century a rival factory called Wedgewood (note the additional "e") also marked its products with its name. Wares by this manufacturer are generally of inferior quality and therefore far less valuable. Wedgwood wares were also imitated on the Continent by factories such as Sèvres, but few fakes are marked.

MARKS

WEDGWOOD
wedgwood

Although early pieces were unmarked, the vast majority of wares made after 1768 were marked "Wedgwood & Bentley", Wedgwood or with initials. From 1860 a system of date coding was used.

▶ LATER WARES
During the 19th century Wedgwood continued to employ some of the leading decorators and designers of the day. This is one of a set of six plates which were painted by A. Walker. The set of plates features fish, which typifies the late 19th-century predilection for naturalistic themes. $150–300 for a single plate

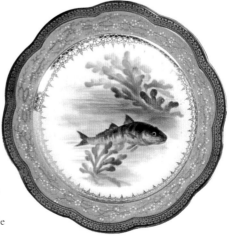

JASPER WARE

INSPIRED BY ANTIQUE CAMEOS AND ROMAN GLASS AND TOMBS, JASPER WARE WAS A FORM OF UNGLAZED STONEWARE INTRODUCED C.1767. IT BECAME ONE OF THE COMPANY'S MOST POPULAR PRODUCTS. THIS PEGASUS VASE WAS MADE IN THE 19TH CENTURY. $7,500-15,000

Many designs were based on drawings by artists of the day such as John Flaxman and inspired by antiquity. These figures illustrate domestic employment and were designed by Elizabeth, Lady Templetown.

The simple cylindrical shape is characteristic of the Neo-classical period.

Jasper ware was made in a variety of colours: green (as here), yellow, lilac, claret, black and white and most commonly blue. Early blue jasper ware was far more distinctive in colour than 20th-century versions: either a very deep purplish blue, or a strong slate blue – not the pale shade nowadays called "Wedgwood" blue.

Cutting of the applied cameo design should be crisp and very refined with a slight translucence in the shallower areas.

QUEENSWARE

Wedgwood's Queensware, a refined type of creamware (see p68), was enormously popular from c.1765 and was generally used for tea and coffee services. Its fame soon spread to Europe, where it proved equally popular and was widely copied. Queensware was named in honour of Queen Charlotte, the wife of King George III. Wares were decorated with moulded designs, transfer prints or hand-painted decoration.

▶ **IMITATIONS**
Wedgwood's success spawned numerous imitations. Among his copyists the most successful was Turner of Lane End; Adam and Spode also made many Wedgwood imitations. This unmarked belt buckle (late 18th early 19th century) may be by Wedgwood but is probably by an imitator such as Turner; if it were marked it would be worth four times as much. $300–450

PRATTWARE

Prattware takes its name from the Pratt family whose pottery in Fenton, Staffordshire developed a distinctive type of lead-glazed earthenware mainly decorated with relief moulding and high-fired colours. Wares of this type were also made in vast quantities by numerous other factories elsewhere in Staffordshire, Yorkshire and Scotland from c.1775–1835. The name Prattware is nowadays a generic term used to describe pearlware earthenwares decorated in a distinctive palette of blue, green, yellow, orange, brown and purple. Themes for the hand-decorated earthenwares included rustic subjects such as milk maids, classical figures, political and royal subjects and animals. Wares include hollow domestic objects and novelty and decorative items such as money boxes and figural groups, and are rarely marked. Value relies heavily on the elaborateness of the decoration and the rarity of the form. Commemorative Prattware is especially popular with today's collectors.

PRATTWARE JUGS

Inky blue, olive-green and ochre, the palette characteristic of most Prattware, was typically used to highlight the low relief-moulded decoration. This baluster jug was made c.1800.

CONDITION

As always damage reduces value. Even with this crack the jug is worth $450–600, but in top condition it would probably fetch 50 percent more. If the subject matter were royalty, value would be even higher.

The jug is adorned with a well-nourished toper sitting in a landscape – a favourite theme c.1800.

HANDLES

The shapes of handles vary; this is very plain but some are far more elaborate in form.

◀ COMMEMORATIVE SUBJECTS

Admiral Rodney is featured on this late 18th century jug, he is typical of the sort of naval and military hero who appear on Prattware jugs. Other figures include Admiral Nelson, Queen Caroline, King George IV, the Duke of York and even Napoleon Bonaparte. $900–1,350

BEWARE

Fake commemorative Prattware jugs have been seen on the market, these are usually recognizable by their softer or weaker colours and over-regular craquelure. Look for signs of genuine wear and tear on the base and only buy from a reputable dealer if you are in doubt.

PRINTED DECORATION

"Prattware" is also the term used to describe a type of stippled colour printing developed by Felix Pratt in the middle of the 19th century. The technique was frequently used to decorate pot lids.

▶ FIGURATIVE GROUPS

Prattware figures such as this dairyman with his cow and dog are more scarce than hollow wares and therefore can command a premium price. This figure probably dates from c.1820; the sponged base is typical of this type of ware, as is the high-temperature palette – blue, orange, green and muddy brown. $1,500–1,800

◀ ORNAMENTS

This "Babes in the Wood" group (c.1820–30) is unusually simply moulded in the manner of late flatbacks. It depicts children against a foliate background and constitutes one of a pair. Such pieces were intended as mantel ornaments and were made by pressing clay into a mould and adding extraneous details by hand. Another popular set of classical figures is composed of "Faith, Hope and Charity". $150–225

LUSTRE

Lustre or metallic decoration, first used in European pottery probably as early as the 13th century in Spain, enjoyed a revival of interest in Britain in the 19th century. Lustre decoration was applied in a variety of ways: either limited to bands or reserves, applied all over or streaked using a "splash" technique. The Wedgwood factory introduced a mottled range called "Moonlight Lustre". Lustre was often used in combination with stencil-printed decoration and is most commonly seen adorning jugs, teapots, mugs and chamber pots. Such objects were produced in numerous potteries in Staffordshire, Sunderland, Wales and Scotland. Lustre is generally available for modest sums although the price increases if the piece is unusually large or decorated with an unusual print.

▶ COMMEMORATIVE LUSTRE

Pink lustre rims were often applied to the rims of white-bodied commemorative wares in the early 19th century. This plate (c.1816) is decorated with a print showing Princess Charlotte and her husband Prince Leopold with Goody Bewley, to whom they later presented a large copy of the Bible – the Princess's kindness was legendary and this subject was a popular one. $375–450

◀ DECORATION

Wares were frequently adorned with a combination of lustre and enamelling. The body of this 19th-century moulded Staffordshire jug is decorated with a landscape in the background, hounds and a colourful trailing vine motif, all of which are highlighted in lustre. Bands of lustre have also been applied on the inside rim, base and handle of the jug. $150–225

▶ COLOURS

Lustre colours depended on the metal oxides which were used and on the colour of body beneath. Pink or purple lustre, which has been used to decorate this chalice (c.1830), was created using a mixture of gold and copper oxides on top of a white body. If gold lustre was applied to a dark body, however, it created a rich bronze colour, while silver was made from platinum oxides. $150–225

BEWARE

Reproductions and fakes of more elaborate pieces of lustre are occasionally seen – look for signs of genuine age.

MARKS

Lustre was produced in many small potteries and few pieces are marked.

IRONSTONE

Ironstone, a type of robust earthenware still produced today, was patented in 1813 by Charles James Mason, a Staffordshire potter. "Mason's ironstone" was a spectacularly successful material for dinner services because it held the heat well and was particularly hardwearing. Mason's was taken over by Ashworth's in 1859 but continued to produce ironstone. Other factories also produced their own versions of the material to which they gave names such as granite china, opaque china and stone china.

Ironstone can form an attractive theme for a collection since pieces are usually decorated in colourful pseudo-Oriental patterns and shapes are often extremely inventive. Jugs cost from $75 while large services can fetch $1,500 or more, depending on the number of pieces.

▶ **SERVICES**
Typically decorated in a colourful Oriental style, this sauce tureen (with cover and stand) and side plate is part of a dinner service (c.1820) containing 95 pieces. The value of the service would be $10,500–12,000

MARKS
Mason's ironstone has an impressed mark; changes in details can help with dating. Spode's impressed mark usually includes the words "New Stone".

◀ **WARES**
Apart from services, ironstone was also used for a range of items large and small, including ornamental vases, jardinières, wine coolers, jugs, teapots, miniature wares, fireplaces, garden seats and card racks such as this example, made c.1820. Rare shapes command a premium and this rack would fetch $675–825.

▶ **SPODE STONE CHINA**
Prior to the introduction of Mason's ironstone, Spode produced a similar material called "stone china" (c.1805). This jug (c.1820) is part of a tea and coffee set containing over 35 pieces; it is decorated with an imitation of a Chinese *famille rose* design. Other makers of similar materials are: Davenport, Minton, Wedgwood, Ridgway, E. & C. Challinor. $375–525

STAFFORDSHIRE FIGURES

In the early 19th century dozens of small potteries in the North Staffordshire region produced a range of decorative pottery figures. The earliest represented idyllic themes: shepherds and shepherdesses, musicians and courting couples were typically brightly enamelled and crisply detailed, with modelling in the round even though they were meant mainly to be seen from one side only. From c.1840 potters began making simpler "flatback" figures, which as their name suggests were not decorated on the reverse. Flatbacks were usually press-moulded and produced in vast numbers in a huge range of subjects, ranging from royal personalities, naval and military heroes, and politicians to criminals, theatrical personalities and animals. Despite their primitive qualities Staffordshire figures have great decorative appeal and enjoy huge popularity with present-day collectors. Prices range from under $150 to $1,500 or more and are affected by the quality of the modelling and enamelling, as well as the subject matter: collectors' favourites include sporting and theatrical subjects and rare and exotic animals like elephants and lions.

◀ **EARLY FIGURES**
A good example of an early Staffordshire group (c.1825). This piece, representing an amorous couple, is well modelled in the round and painted with considerable attention to fashionable detail – note the woman's plumed hat, the height of post-Regency fashion. $1,500–2,250

BEWARE
Numerous fakes and copies of Staffordshire figures have been made, some using original 19th-century moulds. Signs which should arouse suspicion include:
● lighter weight – copies are usually slip-cast from pale chalky clay
● absence of irregularities on the hollow inside made from tools and fingers
● over-regular craquelure – cracking in the glaze should be erratic, if present at all
● deliberately blackened bases.

▲ **COLOURS**
Brilliant enamelling was a feature of early Staffordshire groups and such well-detailed pieces as this are always in demand. The subject of this piece (c.1825–30) depicts a couple being married by a blacksmith – a reference to the New Marriage Act of 1823, which attempted to stop secret marriages. $3,000–4,500

▲ SUBJECTS
Royal personalities were endlessly popular with the Staffordshire potters and these groups of children with dogs (c.1850–60) probably represent the eldest children of

Queen Victoria: the Prince of Wales (later Edward VII) and the Princess Royal. There are numerous different figures of the royal children, some in Scottish dress. $300–450 for the pair

▼ LATER FIGURES
This figure showing Samson wrestling with a lion is probably based on a contemporary circus act like that of Isaac van Ambrugh. In common with most later figures, it is less well modelled and the back is not detailed. The colours are typical of c.1850–60 with strong use of red and ochres. $120–180

◄ DOGS
Spaniels, poodles and greyhounds were among a variety of dogs modelled by the Staffordshire potters and in this example (1860–80) three dogs

surround a fake clock face. The russet colours of the spaniel on the right are instantly recognizable and repeated on hundreds of similar Staffordshire dogs. $180–270

BLUE & WHITE TRANSFER-PRINTED WARE

Although today blue and white transfer-printed wares are avidly collected, when they were first made they were considered little more than utilitarian domestic pieces. Dinner and tea services were made in large numbers and for this reason plates far outnumber other pieces. The decoration was inexpensively produced using underglaze blue transfer prints taken from engraved copper plates and needed only one firing. Different copper plates had to be created for each different size and form produced, and sometimes designs are oddly adapted to fit more unusual shapes. The earliest pieces were inspired by Chinese ceramics; the famous Willow pattern was a pastiche of Oriental design produced by numerous English manufacturers. The heyday of blue and white transfer wares was the late 18th to the mid-19th centuries and pieces made within this period tend to be most sought after. Prices range from $45–75 for a simple plate to $1,500 or more for a large rarity.

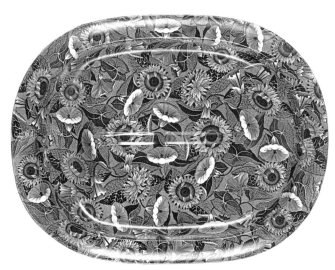

◀ **MANUFACTURERS**
Numerous makers throughout the country produced blue and white wares and while most collectors do not collect by factory, pieces by Spode and Rogers, the main makers, are particularly sought after. This Convolvulus-pattern Spode platter (c.1830) is both decorative and by a top maker so would be worth $1,200–1,350.

▼ **FORMS**
One of the appealing aspects of collecting these wares is the huge range of shapes available – from *bourdaloues* (chamberpots for females) and foot baths, to washstand sets, platters, drainers and tureens. Larger unusual pieces such as this dish (c.1820–25) from a Caramanian sandwich set by Spode (see p79) are always popular. $375–450

WHAT TO LOOK FOR

Other subjects to look out for include:
• eye-catching animals – the Durham Ox is a favourite
• Arctic scenery
• views of Oxford and Cambridge colleges.

REPRODUCTIONS

Fakes are not generally a problem although many of the most popular patterns were produced until the late 19th century; later versions tend to be of inferior quality and are less sought after. Modern reproductions are usually easily identifiable, but beware of a Dr Syntax series made in the 1920s based on 18th-century Rowlandson prints – these are not as old as they may look.

▼ OTHER DESIGNS

This plate (1822–35) features a view of Fair Mount near Philadelphia on a plate by Joseph Stubbs. Many Staffordshire earthenwares intended for export showed American views. $270–360

▲ PATTERNS

Unusual patterns can have a considerable bearing on value. Many were taken from fashionable engravings such as topographical views of foreign scenes. Among the most popular are Spode's Indian Sporting, the design used on this service (c.1820–30), which was based on engravings after Daniel. Caramanian – a series of views of Turkey (see p78) – is also sought after. $270–2,000 per piece

MARKS

Marks do add to value, especially if marked by small makers, but unless made by one of the larger factories with a retail shop most pieces are not marked.

MAJOLICA

Inspired loosely by the Italian low reliefs of della Robbia and the old French pottery of Bernard Palissy, which enjoyed huge popularity during the 19th century, majolica ware was produced in England, Europe and America from the mid-19th century. Majolica was modelled in relief and decorated either with pigments added to the body itself or, more usually, to the glaze. Different parts of the design were painted with coloured pigments which when fired melded together with the glaze. The manufacturer's ability to control the glaze during firing was obviously critical and on poor-quality examples the colours bled together with disastrous effect. Until the 1980s majolica ware was a relatively undervalued market but a prominent exhibition brought its decorative charms to the attentions of interior decorators and prices rose dramatically as a result. At present recent market fluctuations appear to have steadied and the market for good-quality pieces seems as strong and buoyant as ever although buyers are becoming increasingly discerning.

► **MANUFACTURERS** Top factories were Minton, George Jones and Wedgwood, but many other large factories turned their hand to majolica including Royal Worcester and Copeland, as did small manufacturers such as Holdcroft and Brownfield. This c.1875 humorous punchbowl supported by Mr Punch is by George Jones, one of the best 19th-century majolica manufacturers. $6,250–6,750

◄ **DECORATIVE WARES** Novelty domestic wares such as teapots, game tureens and, as here, strawberry sets were typical of the ornamental tablewares made in the 19th century. This double bird set is by George Jones. Majolica was also used for architectural objects such as fountains and wall tiling, jardinières and garden seats. $3,750–5,250

► **VALUE** Big names command a premium as do pieces made in America, even though their quality is inferior to English pieces of similar value. Small unusual pieces are also highly coveted by collectors – a very unusual game tureen can make $30,000 or more, although less exceptional pieces fetch under $1,500. This 1880 Minton hare and duck tureen is of a remarkable design and is worth $30,000–36,000.

▶ **FORMS**
This Wedgwood leaf pickle
stand (c.1880) combines plant
forms with majolica glazes.
Small pieces such as this are
available for modest sums.
$150–225

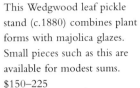

CONDITION
Majolica is particularly prone
to chipping and flaking but
because pieces are bought
primarily for their decorative
appeal value is less
dramatically affected by
damage than for other types
of ceramics and restoration is
fairly common.

▲ **SMALLER MAKERS**
Unmarked majolica or pieces by
less well-known makers can still
attract high prices if the design
is strong. This majolica teapot
(c.1878) is by a smaller maker
but the design reflects the
influence of fashionable
Japanesque styles. $900–1,200

▶ **DECORATION**
High Victorian taste favoured
extraordinarily elaborate
decoration, as seen on this
typical vase of c.1890.
Although rather large it is
unmarked and would therefore
be worth far less than a piece
by Minton. $225–300

REPRODUCTIONS & FAKES
Although fakes are not a major problem some unmarked
pieces have had fake marks added with an etched "Minton"
to boost their value. Modern reproductions are usually
easily identifiable by their lighter potting and their
modelling which is less well-defined.

DOULTON

One of the most prolific and innovative manufacturers of the 19th and 20th centuries, the Doulton factory's success was largely due to the entrepreneurial spirit of Henry Doulton who took over the sole running of the company in 1854. The factory based in Lambeth, London produced utilitarian stonewares such as water filters until 1862 when decorative items, designed by students from the nearby Lambeth School of Art, began to be produced. Over the following decades Doulton established a line in decorated stonewares and employed numerous designers. In 1882

Doulton took over a second factory in Burslem, Staffordshire, where porcelain and earthenware tablewares were produced. The factory became "Royal Doulton" in 1901 and the Burslem factory is still in production although the Lambeth factory closed in 1956. Products are so diverse that collectors often concentrate on wares of a particular type, such as flambé wares, stonewares, faience wares or kingswares. Prices start at around $75 for ornamental wares; the highest prices are commanded by pieces signed by the leading artists of the day, which can fetch over $15,000.

▶ CHINÉ DECORATION
Another popular method of decoration, known as "chiné manner" was patented by Slater for Doulton's. The technique involved pressing lace on to the wet surface of the clay and finishing with hand colouring and gilding. Vast quantities of these wares were made from the 1880s up to 1939 and they remain relatively inexpensive. $75–105

▲ DECORATION
Stonewares were influenced by 16th- and 17th-century designs and often feature incised or applied and hand-carved decoration. Motifs such as beaded borders are typical characteristics as is the restrained palette in shades of blue and brown. This 1879 jug by Florence Barlow and Emma Martin is typically decorated with beaded roundels and paler scrolling foliage. $180–270

◀ HANNAH BARLOW
Deer provide a recurring decorative theme in Hannah Barlow's work, but the *pâte sur pâte* decoration on this vase (made c.1885 at the Lambeth factory) is unusual and was added by William Baron, who later set up his own pottery in Devon (see p86). $450–600

MARKS
Wares are marked with the name of the factory, impressed, printed or painted; they are also marked with the initials of the artist and the date.

DOULTON DESIGNERS

NAME	SPECIALITY	MARKS
George Tinworth	Speciality modelling, religious plaques, frog and mice groups	GT + Doulton
Hannah Barlow	Incised decoration, animal subjects	BHB + Doulton
Florence Barlow	Incised bird subjects	FEB + Doulton
Frank Butler	Bold shapes, decorated with natural forms	FAB + Doulton
Harry Nixon	Song and Chang, flambé wares	H Nixon (on side of piece generally)
Mark V Marshall	Well-modelled stoneware – worked with Martin Brothers	MVM
Eliza Simmance	High-quality Art Nouveau designs	ES

▼ **SONG WARE**
Inspired by Chinese ceramics Royal Doulton's Song wares came in a choice of subjects and colourways. This "Song" vase (c.1920) by Arthur Charles Eaton is painted with a typically exotic bird. $1,800–2,250

▲ **MICE GROUPS**
Among the most popular novelties for which George Tinworth is famed are novelty mice groups (c.1890) such as this which shows mice playing instruments. Tinworth also produced frog groups and imp musicians which are equally popular. $1,050–1,350

MARTIN WARE

One of the most original "studio" potteries of the 19th century was established by the Martin brothers in a studio in Fulham and later in Southall, London. There were four brothers, Robert Wallace, Charles Douglas, Walter Frazer and Edwin Bruce. Robert Wallace, a sculptor and the firm's leading creative force, was fascinated by the grotesque gargoyles he encountered while working as an apprentice on the Houses of Parliament, and was responsible for the introduction of the extraordinary bird jars with movable heads, known as "Wally" birds, that are among the company's most distinctive and individual wares. The company also made jugs and mugs with faces on each side, vases, some in the form of naturalistic gourds, ordinary jugs and other ornamental pieces.

▶ **BIRDS**
Martin Brothers' birds reflect the Victorian fascination with the grotesque and their quirky features were often based on people the brothers knew personally. These examples were made in the late 19th or early 20th century, and like most others of their type have removable heads. Value is affected by size; large pieces are worth $12,000–15,000, while smaller examples would fetch around $3,000–4,500.

MARKS
Pieces are usually incised "R W Martin Bros, London & Southall" and dated. Early pieces may just be signed "Martin".

BEWARE

Martinware has enjoyed huge popularity and fakes do appear on the market, but these are usually identifiable by their lack of subtlety in decoration and modelling. Although it has a Martin "signature" this spoon warmer in the shape of a tortoise is far inferior in its modelling and clearly a fake. Fakes have sometimes been made by taking a mould from an original piece; hence the marks are also moulded. This should indicate to the prospective buyer that the piece has been faked.

▲ **TILES**
Tiles are among the Martin Brothers' more unusual products; the fish with which this panel (c.1890) is decorated are also seen on vases. $4,500–6,000

WILLIAM de MORGAN

One of the most important figures in the Arts and Craft movement, de Morgan was employed as a designer by William Morris before he set up his own business. De Morgan specialized in producing tiles and lustre wares, inspired by Islamic and Hispano-Moresque ceramics, and in "Persian" wares based on Turkish pottery designs. Among the leading decorators he employed were Fred and Charles Passenger and Joe Juster, all of whom often signed pieces with their initials rather than with the de Morgan mark. De Morgan's highly decorative wares have a ready following and can fetch very high sums. "Persian" pieces fetch $3,000 or more according to size and choice of decoration. Tiles start at around $75 for 6in (15cm) sizes in the most usual patterns, many of which were produced for fireplace surrounds; 8in (20cm) tiles with an unusual pattern can fetch $750 or more.

▶ "PERSIAN" WARES

Among the most distinctive and valuable pieces of de Morgan pottery are Persian-inspired wares such as this vase (c.1880). It has been painted by leading decorator Fred Passenger with peacocks and formalized flowers. The vivid turquoise and green shades and stylized floral decoration are based on those found on Persian and Iznik pottery. $15,000–18,000

▶ DECORATION

Full-masted galleons and stylized fish were favourite de Morgan motifs; here dolphins and a galleon combine on a vase (c.1890) made in ruby lustre, for which de Morgan is also famed. A range of triple lustre glazes known as "Moonlight" and "Sunset suite" are the most complex and valuable of all de Morgan's lustre wares. $7,500–9,000

MARKS

An impressed or painted mark with the name of the company is usually found, frequently in conjunction with a motif such as an abbey, a tulip or a rose. The motifs relate to the period and location of the various factory sites de Morgan established.

▶ TILES

De Morgan produced tiles (c.1890) in a wide range of styles and patterns and prices depend on decorative appeal and size. Although elaborately decorated these 6in (15cm) tiles are less expensive than if they formed part of a large decorative panel. $150–600 each

DEVON POTTERIES

The discovery of deposits of high-quality red clay suitable for making fine terracotta wares together with a burgeoning tourist industry and a growing demand for souvenirs, encouraged a handful of small potteries to set up in Devon in the mid- to late 19th century. In 1869 the Watcombe Terracotta Company began producing painted wares and unglazed pieces decorated with turquoise borders and glazed interiors. The Torquay Terracotta Company made figurative subjects, painted wares and ceramics in the style of the Aesthetic movement. Another South Devon pottery was Aller Vale which made wares decorated with incised mottoes such as jugs

and teapots as well as now obsolete objects such as plaques for resting curling tongs. In North Devon near Fremington Edwin Beer Fishley produced pottery simply decorated with coloured slips or incised designs. Another important pottery located at Barnstaple was C. H. Brannam, which became well known for its "Royal Barum" ware. The company's reputation grew in the 1880s when it began selling through Liberty's, London, and later pieces are in general more elaborately coloured and more varied. Decorators include James Dewdney and William Leonard Baron; the latter eventually set up his own pottery in Barnstaple too.

◀ **VASES**
Among the most expensive pieces of Devon pottery are those decorated in the style of the Aesthetic movement – such as this pair of vases made c.1878 by the Torquay Terracotta Company.

The vases, designed by Louis F. Day and painted by Alexander Fisher (senior) to represent "morning" and "night", are worth $3,000–4,500 but less spectacular examples sell from $150.

VALUES
Prices vary considerably but these features are desirable:
• pieces in artistic styles
• large sculptural pieces
• large slip-decorated vases.

▶ **ALLER VALE**
Pixies proved to be a popular motif with tourists; this pixie-adorned jug (late 19thC) was made by the Aller Vale pottery, one of the most prolific of the Devon potteries that later merged with Watcombe. $120–180

▶ **C. H. BRANNAM**
Although the birds and floral roundels that decorate this jug (c.1910) are heavily influenced by Oriental ceramics, the use of incised decoration in conjunction with coloured slips is typical of the Brannam pottery. $225–300

▲ **TERRACOTTA FIGURES**
Unglazed terracotta figures were a popular product of the Watcombe and Torquay Terracotta companies in the late 19th century. This angel made by the Torquay Terracotta Company is typical of the religious subjects produced there. Portrait busts, classical subjects and figural groups were also produced. $180–270

▼ **SOUVENIRS**
Among the less expensive tourist souvenirs produced in the Devon studios some surprising novelty items can be found. This Baron of Barnstaple pottery bell (c.1920) is modelled in the form of a female head. It carries a rather dubious inscription – "The perfect woman speaks only when tolled." $120–180

MARKS

The marks most commonly found on Devon pottery include:

- **"Aller Vale"** impressed name or incised hand-written signature mark
- **"Torquay Terracotta Co"** initials or name in full
- **"Watcombe"** usually a printed mark.

A millennium after the development of porcelain in the Far East the tantalizing secret of how to make it was still undiscovered by European potters. By the late 16th century, as Portuguese traders began to export Oriental porcelain to Europe, demand outstripped supply, prompting European potters to try to discover the elusive formula. Although various factories in France and England managed to make soft-paste porcelain in the 17th century, it was not until 1708 that a German alchemist, Johann Friedrich Böttger, found a formula for hard-paste porcelain. In 1710 the Meissen factory opened near Dresden; it dominated porcelain production for the next 50 years or so, but as the secret leaked out, factories such as Vienna, Fürstenberg and Nymphenburg began hard-paste production too.

In due course, Meissen's preeminence was challenged by the French royal porcelain manufactory of Sèvres, which began making wares with spectacular coloured grounds and raised gilding of unrivalled quality. Many of the most famous European factories continued to produce porcelain throughout the 19th century and beyond, although from the mid-19th century few new ideas and styles evolved and most production remained heavily retrospective until after World War I, when some factories began producing refreshingly innovative designs.

For collectors European porcelain offers a vast range of prices and objects, from modestly priced cups and saucers to elaborate figurative groups.

EARLY MEISSEN

Meissen's earliest wares included a type of red stoneware called jasper ware, which is extremely rare and valuable, and porcelain decorated in Oriental style. In 1720 the factory was joined by J. G. Herold, a skilful chemist who developed a new range of colours, and in the 1730s by J. J. Kaendler who was a brilliant modeller. During this period painted decoration became more European in style and modelling became an increasingly important part of the overall decoration.

▲ **TEAWARES**
Tea and coffee drinking were fashionable among the wealthy and aristocratic classes in the 18th century, and large quantities of wares survive. This teabowl (c.1725) is a good example of Meissen's early fascination with chinoiserie decoration. $3,000–4,500

MARKS
Beware The Meissen mark was copied by numerous other leading factories in Europe and England and is certainly no guarantee of authenticity. The crossed swords are more usually alone. The "KPM" mark is only used on grand early pieces pre-1740.

MEISSEN SAUCERS

THIS TYPICAL MEISSEN SAUCER MADE C.1760 WAS ORIGINALLY PART OF A TEA AND COFFEE SERVICE ALL DECORATED IN THE SAME PATTERN. SAUCERS ON THEIR OWN ARE GENERALLY INEXPENSIVE AND POPULAR WITH COLLECTORS AS THEY ARE EASY TO DISPLAY. $150–225

The modest gilding is a characteristic of much early German porcelain.

The idyllic landscape subject and the absence of a frame around the painting are also typical Rococo features.

The reverse side would be marked in the usual way with the crossed swords and possibly with an impressed number.

Monochrome decoration was fashionable in the mid-18th century; puce was particularly popular in the Rococo period.

▲ COLOURED GROUNDS

Coloured grounds were introduced in the latter 1720s and always command a premium with collectors. The turquoise ground on this faceted ovoid teapot (c.1735) reflects the colour of Chinese celadon; other colours you might come across include yellow, claret and dark blue. $4,500–6,000

▼ FIGURES

Figural groups made up a large part of Meissen's output, and this shepherd and shepherdess (c.1740) are typical of the decorative subjects in which the factory excelled. $2,250–3,000

19TH- & 20TH-CENTURY MEISSEN

During the early 19th century Meissen, in common with many other leading European porcelain manufacturers, produced elaborately decorated and gilded pieces in the prevailing Empire style. Painted decoration became increasingly elaborate, with the surface treated as a canvas and adorned with romantic topographical views or Classical subjects. As the century progressed the factory concentrated on repetitions of 18th-century designs and this revivalist trend continued until the 1920s when designers such as Paul Scheurich and von Lowenich began to produce imaginative modern pieces. Although less sought after by serious collectors 19th-century Meissen has obvious decorative appeal.

▶ **STYLES**
Pierced work had been made from the mid–18th century but became increasingly popular from the 1820s as part of the fashion for Rococo style. The deeply modelled contours of trailing flowers with small floral cartouches that adorn this ornamental basket (c.1840) are typical of the 19th century's love of opulent decoration. $600–900

◀ **HUNTING THEMES**
The hunt proved a popular theme in the 1760s and continued to inspire many German factories in the following century. This base of this figure (c.1880) is perhaps more elaborate than an 18th-century example, and it is larger in scale. $3,000–4,500

▶ **SUBJECTS**
Scenes based on classical antiquity were popular in the late 19th century and this scene showing Europa and the Bull is after a painting by Boucher. The blue and gilded border reflects the style made popular by Sèvres. Wares of this type were copied by many other European factories in the late 19th century. It is their decorative appeal rather than their rarity that makes them sought after. $600–900

◄ FIGURES
This figurative group
contains a typical
19th-century cocktail
of decorative styles:
elements of Neo-
classicism in the border
and urn; and the rustic
naturalism of the
Rococo period in the
base and costumes.
The slightly fiddly,
detailed costumes are
also characteristic of
the 19th century.
$1,500–2,250

► FORMS
Forms became more
complex at the end of
the 19th century, and
decoration often
features a confusion
of different styles.
In this example
Watteauesque scenes,
first made popular
between c.1740 and
1745, are teamed with
stylized flowers typical
of a later period and
the vase's shape is
clearly derived from
Classical prototypes.
$3,000–4,500

**◄ 20TH-CENTURY
MEISSEN**
One of the most
innovative designers
working at Meissen in
the 1930s, Professor
Paul Scheurich
specialized in figures
with elongated limbs
and decadent poses in
the Art Deco style and
his work commands
high prices. This
group of a woman
and Moor is modelled
and decorated with
typical refinement and
delicacy. $3,750–5,250

OTHER GERMAN FACTORIES

Within a few decades of Meissen's discovery of the secret of porcelain-making, a potent mixture of greed and treachery helped to spread the formula throughout Europe and by the mid-18th century a handful of other German factories had been established. Among the most important of these were Höchst, Frankenthal, Ludwigsburg and Nymphenburg. Other less prolific factories included Fulda and Fürstenberg. Although

FRANKENTHAL	HÖCHST
A Frankenthal group of shepherd and flock, 1773. $6,000–7,500 |
Children playing by J. P. Melchior, c.1767 $2,250–3,000 |

	FRANKENTHAL	HÖCHST
CHARACTERISTICS	• Shallow rounded base with shallow Rococo scrolls broadly washed in gilding • Mound encrusted with mossy shavings of porcelain • Fine white body	• Very pale yellow, pink and blue details • Simple grassy mound base with brown streaks • Sweet plump childish faces • Creamy body
KEY MODELLERS	• Johann Friedrich Lück • J. W. Lanz • Conrad Linck	• J. P. Melchior • Johann Friedrich Lück • Laurentius Russinger
MARKS	• Initials "CT" in underglaze blue • Sometimes numbers to show year of production	• Wheel mark, usually in underglaze blue, also in purple or blue • Incised numbers and letters sometimes

the factories produced a similar range of products, many based on designs first developed by Meissen, each developed its characteristic style and used distinctive paste, and some knowledge of both can help with identification. Of the smaller factories' output pieces made by Nymphenburg are particularly refined and correspondingly expensive, but all factories tend to have a keen following among porcelain collectors.

LUDWIGSBURG	NYMPHENBURG	
A group of dancers by J. Nees, c.1765. $6,000–9,000	Figure of a female dancer, c.1760. $12,000–18,000	
• Stiffly posed figures; faces have long bridgeless noses and doll-like features • Notched deeply modelled base • Subdued pastel palette • Smoky, greyish glaze	• Sophisticated handling of porcelain • Subtle Rococo pose with upwardly spiralling movement • Elongated bodies, delicate faces with slightly exaggerated expressions • Creamy coloured lightweight slip-cast body	CHARACTERISTICS
• Joseph Nees • Johann Beyer • J. H. von Damiecher	• F. A. Bustelli • J. P. Melchior • D. J. Auliczek (famous for hunting scenes)	KEY MODELLERS
• Interlaced Cs with coronet or a staghorn mark: three in a shield or one separate	• An impressed or incised shield mark often prominently placed at front of base	MARKS

BERLIN & LATER GERMAN FACTORIES

Berlin's first factory, founded in 1752 by W. K. Wegely, closed only five years later. In 1761 King Frederick the Great, together with a financier, established a second factory which the King later took sole charge of, succeeded by the State; this factory survives to the present day. Berlin porcelain of the 18th century is extremely rare and you are far more likely to come across 19th-century pieces, exquisitely decorated with detailed panels on solid coloured grounds, which are easily confused with porcelain made around the same time in Vienna and Paris. The Berlin factory also produced quantities of porcelain plaques, many of which were independently decorated with copies of well-known paintings. During the 19th and early 20th centuries the area near Meissen surrounding the city of Dresden became a major German centre of porcelain production with numerous factories producing ornamental and tea and dinner services in the style of Meissen and Sèvres.

◄ VALUE
Berlin and Dresden porcelain is widely available at a range of prices depending on the usual criteria of size, subject and decorative appeal. Pieces such as this Berlin *solitaire* (c.1775), beautifully painted in puce with Watteauesque figures in landscape vignettes, reflect the Rococo taste for monochrome decoration and no frames. $10,500–13,500

► TOPOGRAPHICAL & CITY VIEWS
Topographical and city views were a speciality of Berlin and Viennese porcelain decorators from the early 19th century. Scenes such as the one of the Gross Schloss decorating this egg are often named and among the most finely detailed of those produced anywhere in Europe. Earlier examples have either rectilinear or formal borders. The neo-Rococo gilt borders here indicate a date c.1880. Small decorative items like the egg shown here are rather unusual; plates and cabinet cups and saucers are much more readily available to collectors at lower prices. $1,500–3,000

FIGURES
A range of figures based on Meissen models was made by Wegely. The second factory made a series called "The Cries of Berlin", modelled by the Meyer brothers.

▶ **PORCELAIN PLAQUES**
Popular paintings by artists such as Watteau, Murillo and Richter provided the subjects for huge numbers of porcelain plaques manufactured in Berlin. Ladies were favourite subjects too; this plaque shows a copy of a portrait of Beatrice Cenci by Guido Reni (c.1880). $3,000–4,500

▶ **DECORATION**
Snowball vases or *Schneeballen*, decorated with May blossom, were first made by Meissen in the 18th century, but several 19th-century factories continued the tradition by covering the entire surface of objects with tiny florets. This large unmarked vase could be made by a number of factories in the Dresden area. $1,500–4,500

◀ **CARL THIEME**
A brilliant example of the 19th-century love of excessive ornament, this baluster vase was made by Carl Thieme, one of the major manufacturers in the Dresden area. Pieces such as this are obviously extremely vulnerable to damage and small chips are acceptable. $3,000–4,500

VIENNA

Vienna was the second European factory to begin producing hard-paste porcelain. The factory was founded by Claudius Innocentius du Pacquier, who bribed and cajoled the secret from various disgruntled Meissen employees. Until the 1780s Vienna produced a similar range of wares to those made by Meissen, but figures were rarer and more stiffly modelled. In 1744 the company was taken over by the State and the hitherto limited production increased in quantity. In 1784 a new director was appointed and the factory began producing wares in the Neo-classical style, with elaborate painted scenes and heavy gilding of very similar appearance to wares from centres such as Berlin and St Petersburg. The Vienna factory closed in 1864 but many imitations of its more elaborate wares were produced in the late 19th century.

Porcelain from the du Pacquier period is rare, and consequently prices start at around $2,250. Also highly desirable are pieces from later periods decorated by sought-after painters such as Joseph Nigg, a famous flower painter. Prices for other late pieces are chiefly dependent on their decorative appeal.

◀ **DECORATION**
The use of solid gilt grounds became more prevalent at the turn of the 18th century and was used by all leading factories from Paris to St Petersburg. This coffee cup is decorated with a combination of Classical key border and informal Rococo scattered flowers.
$600–900

DU PACQUIER PORCELAIN
Porcelain from the du Pacquier period (1719–44) is rarer than Meissen and few pieces have survived. It is similar in composition to early Meissen and often has a greenish tone. Wares are usually decorated with chinoiserie and very formal Baroque strapwork borders. Dominant colours are puce, iron red and monochromes. Compared with Meissen the manner of painting is naive. Figures are rare and idiosyncratic.

▲ **WARES**
Although tablewares made up the bulk of the factory's output it also made some enchanting accessories such as this exquisite travelling casket (c.1785), decorated in French style with a dotted green ground.
$4,500–7,500

▲ LATER "VIENNA-STYLE" WARES
After 1864 other European factories continued to produce wares in similar style. This vase and cover, one of a pair decorated with scenes of Galatea, and Europa and the Bull within seeded gilt lines, are late 19th-century pastiches of Vienna wares of the early 19th century. Less sensitively painted than the genuine article, they are worth a fraction of the price. $900–1,050 for the pair

▼ STYLES
The landscape subject within formal borders shows the transition between the decorative Rococo and the nascent Neo-classical styles. *Tête à têtes* (small teasets or cabarets) containing enough pieces for two became fashionable in the mid-18th century as part of the trend for boudoir intimacy. $1,000–27,000 for 8 pieces

▲ TOPOGRAPHICAL SCENES
Topographical scenes were one of the specialities of Viennese decorators and the scenes were often named on the base. This cabinet cup and saucer (c.1830) is decorated with a named view of Schönbrunn palace. $1,800–2,250

ITALY

Italy was the first European country to try to produce porcelain and began experimenting in the 16th century. In 1575 Duke Francesco de Medici opened a short-lived factory in Florence but the first successful porcelain factory, Vezzi, was not established until 1720, when a former Meissen employee, Christoph Hunger, stole the formula and took it to Venice. Other leading factories at Doccia and Cozzi soon followed suit and the most famous Italian porcelain of all was made from 1743 at Capodimonte, Naples. When Naples fell under Spanish rule the Capodimonte factory moved to Buen Retiro in Spain, but returned to Naples in the late 18th century. Some Italian porcelain is characterized by its greyish granular appearance and is easily confused with pieces from minor German factories. Prices tend to be comparatively high and there is a strong home market. The most readily available pieces tend to be from Doccia, mostly in the quasi-Oriental or Neo-classical style.

MARKS

- The most common mark is the red or gold anchor of Cozzi – this is much bigger than the similar Chelsea mark.
- Capodimonte use a fleur-de-lis mark, usually in underglaze blue or gold.
- After 1757 Doccia marked with this star; a red, blue or gold "F" is used 1792–1815.

▼ **IDENTIFICATION**
The rather delicate but primitive brushwork decorating this teacup and saucer is similar to Kakiemon styles of the 1740s. The angular scrolled handle is characteristic of the Capodimonte factory and can be found on coffee pots and other similar wares.
$2,250–3,000

▲ **CAPODIMONTE**
This figure of a pug (c.1750) is a copy of a Meissen original by J. J. Kaendler of c.1740. Reinterpreted in the soft-paste porcelain of Capodimonte, the crisp details are to a great extent lost but this would still be worth more than the Meissen original.
$6,000–9,000

FIGURES

Italian factories made a range of figures dressed in a variety of ways. A classical subject is less desirable than a group in contemporary dress, and pieces should always be in good condition.

◀ **SHAPES**
The forms used by Italian porcelain-makers are often idiosyncratic and distinctive from those used by factories elsewhere in Europe. This Doccia coffee pot (made c.1775) combines an early baluster form, an oddly shaped spout and a shallow domed cover with Neo-classical decoration. The tentative, fussy gilding is also characteristic of much Italian porcelain. $7,500–12,000

▶ **DECORATION**
One feature of late 18th- and 19th-century decoration is the use of relief-moulded decoration. This small covered beaker, made by the Cozzi factory c.1780, is decorated with the low-relief lion of Venice. $1,200–1,800

◀ **NAPLES**
Neo-classical decoration was very popular on Neapolitan porcelain of the late 18th century and this coffee can and saucer (c.1790) are no exception. Fashionably decorated with Classical figures on a black ground panel, they boast borders of palmettes and swags which are also derived from antiquity. These ornaments are most probably inspired by the local archeological excavations at Herculaneum and Pompeii on the Bay of Naples. $3,750–5,250

EARLY FRENCH PORCELAIN

The first French factory to produce porcelain successfully was at St Cloud, near Paris, in the 1690s, although some was probably made at Rouen earlier. Among the other early factories who followed suit in the 18th century, the most important were Chantilly and Mennecy. French factories produced tablewares and figures as well as a range of small decorative objects such as snuff boxes, *étuis* and *nécessaires*. Decorative styles and good proportion were influenced by Chinese and Japanese ceramics, although some slightly later pieces also reflect fashions introduced by Meissen. Until 1769 all porcelain produced in France was soft paste (see p26) and compared with German porcelain of the same date it looks softer and creamier. Pieces are often unmarked and can be difficult to attribute as factories often changed the pastes they used. In general, 18th-century French porcelain is less widely available than that made by leading German factories. While prices tend to reflect this relative rarity the naive quality of the French product (except Sèvres) tends to make it slightly less expensive than more sophisticated pieces of the same date made in Germany.

> **BEWARE**
> Chantilly's distinctive style was imitated in the 19th century by Samson of Paris – and sometimes the original Samson marks have been removed. Samson however used hard-paste porcelain, and pieces look harder and shinier compared to true soft paste.

▲ ST CLOUD
This snuff box is typical of the range of small decorative items produced in France in the 18th century. Many of these objects have metal mounts which may, as in the case of this one, bear marks that can help with dating. The white cat shows the influence of *blanc de Chine* – uncoloured, thickly glazed Chinese porcelain produced from the Ming dynasty onwards. St Cloud paste is greyish-white and often peppered with black flecks.
$3,000–4,500

▼ CHANTILLY
The patron of the Chantilly factory was the Prince de Condé, a passionate collector of Kakiemon, and most of the factory's wares reflect his taste for the exotic. The flowers decorating this *bonbonnière* reflect this favourite style and indicate that it was probably made at Chantilly.
$4,500–7,500

► **GILDING**
This Chantilly cachepot (c.1750) is decorated with a rustic European landscape inspired perhaps by Meissen. In common with most early French porcelain (and unlike 18th-century German porcelain) it is not gilded. Flower pots and cachepots were especially popular at Chantilly and Sèvres.

The pleated contours and the handles applied with flowers are characteristic, as is the subtle delicate brushwork. This factory used tin glaze, perhaps to hide defects in the clay and to improve the surface, and consequently wares may often have a somewhat opaque appearance. $3,000–4,500

MARKS
- **St Cloud** variations of this mark are found in blue and red or impressed.
- **Chantilly** the hunting horn mark is used in red, black and blue. Rarely the word "Chantilly" appears.
- **Mennecy** the initials "DV" for Duc de Villeroy, patron of Mennecy, were used, sometimes with a crown above.

◄ **MENNECY**
This (c.1755–60) rather stiff and puppet-like pair of Mennecy figures are typically naively modelled and are painted in soft, rather washed-out colours, with the predominant use of pastel blue, irregularly streaked pink and yellow.

Faces typically lack detail. The factory produced an extensive range of tea and coffee services, decorative wares such as vases, and figures. Figures of peasants and traders are available from $3,000 and upwards, but exotic subjects such as these are usually much more valuable. $7,500–12,000 for the pair

VINCENNES & SÈVRES

France's most famous porcelain factory, Sèvres, started life at Vincennes near Fontainebleau, where in 1738 a new factory began to produce soft-paste porcelain. In 1756 the factory moved to Sèvres, near the home of one of its keenest patrons, Louis XV's mistress Madame de Pompadour; soon after, the King became the owner of the factory. After 1769 Sèvres began making hard-paste porcelain (as well as soft paste) and after c.1803 stopped making soft paste completely.

Sèvres porcelain is famed for its lavish gilding and brilliantly coloured grounds, which formed a framework for panels decorated with flowers, figure subjects or landscapes. Its illustrious reputation has however attracted numerous imitators. Marks and styles were copied throughout Europe and confusion also arises because at the time of the French Revolution the factory was taken over by the state and numerous pieces were sold in the white to independent decorators in France and England. Coloured grounds are prone to faking; probably about 90 percent of all *bleu céleste* pieces, in the delicate sky blue for which Sèvres is known, are imitations.

MARKS

The interlaced Sèvres Ls were centred with a date letter from 1753. This is one of the most commonly faked of all porcelain marks. Look for strong definition on genuine pieces – a weak and attenuated mark is usually suspect.

▶ **VINCENNES**
All Vincennes and Sèvres forms are known by special names; this double-handled vase, made c.1755, is called a vase *Duplessis à fleurs* – after the celebrated sculptor employed by the factory to create interesting shapes. This colour, called *bleu céleste*, was the most popular of all coloured grounds – and also the most commonly faked. Pieces from the Vincennes period are rare and therefore command a premium. $7,500–12,000

▲ **COLOURS**
The brilliant shade of green used for this tea caddy (c.1780) was another of Sèvres' most distinctive colours. The range of coloured grounds was gradually introduced in the 18th century. Knowledge of these colours can help with dating and spotting fakes (see p24), since some pastiches combine late colours with early date marks. Green was introduced in 1756. Other Sèvres colours include: *bleu lapis* (lapis blue), 1749; *bleu céleste* (sky blue), 1752; *jaune jonquille* (pastel yellow), 1753; *violette* (violet), 1757; *rose* (pink), 1758; *bleu royal* (royal blue), 1763. $3,000– 4,500

BISCUIT FIGURES

The Vincennes and Sèvres factories also produced a range of unglazed porcelain figures modelled by E. M. Falconet, often after the designs of François Boucher. This type of porcelain is known as biscuit. Until recently these figures remained relatively inexpensive although they have risen considerably in value in the last few years.

◀ **GILDING**
Sèvres gilding is invariably soft and richly applied and the factory developed a wide range of distinctive techniques. This coffee can and saucer (made 1768) are decorated with the popular *œil-de-*
perdrix (partridge eye) gilded decoration; *caillouté* (pebble) decoration was another favourite pattern; while on some pieces gilding was raised and tooled to create detailed bouquets of flowers and foliage. $1,200–1,800

▼ **DECORATION & FORM**
Monochrome decoration as on this tea service was less commonly used at Sèvres than in German factories but
the shapes of the pear-shaped jug with tripod feet and ovoid teapot with ear-shaped handle are absolutely typical of 18th-century Sèvres forms. $7,500–10,500

◀ **LATER SÈVRES**
Like other leading European factories in the early 19th century Sèvres began producing more formally decorated pieces using semi-mechanical methods of
gilding. This pale blue (*bleu agate*) tea service is made from hard-paste porcelain and looks much harder and sharper than the earlier pieces illustrated on these pages. $2,750–3,000

LATER FRENCH PORCELAIN

From the late 18th century and throughout the first half of the 19th Paris blossomed as a centre of porcelain manufacture as dozens of factories and enamelling shops began producing dinner services, teawares and ornamental pieces for the newly affluent population. As the 19th century progressed, the rising costs of running a commercial factory in the capital encouraged many manufacturers to move to the countryside near Limoges, where labour was cheaper and raw materials were readily available. Most French factories of this time have little individual style, relying heavily on earlier designs from Sèvres and elsewhere for inspiration. All factories produced only hard-paste porcelain (although some also made pottery) and marked their wares erratically. Many unmarked pieces and pieces with spurious Sèvres marks also survive; these are often catalogued either as "Paris" or as "Sèvres style". Prices depend heavily on the size and decorative appeal of the subject. Small plates are available for under $450, while large decorative vases can cost $1,500 or more.

◀ **DECORATIVE WARES**
Metal-mounted vases and covers are typical of the decorative items produced from the mid-19th century. The figurative panel, probably copied from a painting by Boucher or Watteau, is set against a dark blue ground – probably the most popular of all coloured grounds at this time. $3,000–4,500

IMPORTANT 19TH-CENTURY FRENCH FACTORIES
Sèvres continued to be France's best-known porcelain factory, but other leading names included:
● **Paris** Jacob Petit, Dagoty & Honoré, Darte Frères, Discry, Talmour, Pouyat, Nast, Clignancourt
● **Limoges** Denuelle, Michel & Valin, Alluaud, Ardant, Gibus & Cie, Jouhanneaud & Dubois, Haviland, Ruaud

MARKS
As with many pieces of this type the vase above is marked only with imitation Sèvres marks; few pieces are marked by their manufacturer, and some are not even porcelain. If genuine marks do appear they are usually of the overglaze, stencilled or printed varieties.

▲ **PICTORIAL SUBJECTS**
Scale and ostentation were typical of many of the decorative items produced at this time and pictorial plates featuring Louis XVI and Marie Antoinette were especially popular after c.1850. Many of the portraits on plates such as these were transfer-printed and then enamelled over. Their value lies chiefly in their decorative appeal. $450–750

◀ **THEMES**
The fashion for Egyptian subjects, a hallmark of French Empire style in the early decades of the 19th century, was fuelled by Napoleon's campaigns in North Africa. This elaborate centrepiece is adorned with characteristic sphinxes supporting a basket bordered with lotus petals. Both stylish and large (measuring 18in [46cm] high) this piece would command a high price in the market. Smaller pieces would cost a fraction of the price. $6,000–7,500

▶ **TEA SETS**
Among the wide range of tea sets produced at this time were cabarets – small tea sets usually for two also known as *tête à têtes* (see below) and *solitaires* for one.

This late 19th-century cabaret is painted with 18th-century court beauties and includes a teapot, large sugar bowl, jug, cup and saucer and matching tray. $900–1,200

◀ **VALUE**
Quality and an illustrious provenance can dramatically affect the value of porcelain. Painted in a tasteful *grisaille* (grey monochrome), the decoration of this *tête à tête* made c.1785 by the Paris factory of the Duc d'Angoulême is highly refined, and the set has a royal history: it was a gift from Marie Antoinette to a Swedish count. $3,750–4,500

SWITZERLAND

In Switzerland a porcelain factory founded in 1763 at Scoren near Zurich by the painter Salomon Gessner continued to produce wares until the late 19th century. The factory began by producing soft-paste porcelain but by 1765 this was replaced by hard paste. Wares include tea and coffee services as well as a wide range of figures which are often recognizable by their rather static poses. Painted decoration tends to follow fashions established elsewhere in Europe although the style in which flowers and landscapes are painted is often sparse and stiff. The hard paste used by the factory tends to be greyish in colour and sugary in texture, and has a glassy greyish glaze. Colours before 1780 are typically soft though after this date a strong russet and yellow were introduced. Although Swiss porcelain is less widely available than that made by major German and French factories, it is not too scarce and remains popular with Swiss and other European collectors. Values are similar to those for smaller German factories, with the highest prices being paid for early rarities.

▶ **WARES**
This pair of Zurich dinner plates (c.1770) have obvious similarities with pieces made in Germany, but the figures are more stiffly painted and the three scattered landscapes on the rims would be unusual on German porcelain. The gilt dentil (indented) rims are also highly characteristic of Swiss porcelain. $5,250–6,750

▼ **VALUES**
Teabowls and saucers, such as this made c.1770, are among the most affordable pieces of 18th-century Swiss porcelain. The estuary scenes which decorate these examples are populated with Oriental figures – a reflection of the taste for chinoiserie. $450–750

MARKS
Pieces are usually marked with a "Z" incised or in underglaze blue. Dots and incised letters and numbers are also sometimes found.

▶ MINIATURES

The Zurich factory also produced a range of miniature figures which are usually more affordably priced than larger subjects. These figures of a song seller and a fisherwoman (c.1770) measure about 4in (10cm); most figures are about twice this size. $1,200–1,800 each figure

FIGURE SUBJECTS

Among the range of subjects produced by the Zurich factory, those you might come across include:
- street vendors
- fisherfolk
- musicians
- craftsmen
- fashionable ladies and gentlemen
- classical figures
- hunters
- shepherds and shepherdesses

FIGURES

THE ZURICH FACTORY PRODUCED A WIDE RANGE OF FIGURES THROUGHOUT THE 18TH CENTURY. THIS GIRL WITH A BROKEN POT, MODELLED BY VALENTIN SONNENSCHEIN C.1775, HAS MANY OF THE FEATURES YOU WOULD LOOK FOR ON A SWISS FIGURE. $3,750–4,500

Lack of detail in the face is a typical feature.

Soft autumnal or pastel shades are invariably found.

The modelling is so loose that the hard paste almost looks like soft paste.

Modelling of details such as hands and costume is very rudimentary.

Simple bases with little decoration are found on most Zurich figures.

The piece is marked with a blue "Z" and two dots.

OTHER PORCELAIN CENTRES – DENMARK & LOW COUNTRIES

The first porcelain factory was established in Copenhagen in 1760 with the help of German craftsmen from Meissen and Fürstenberg. The factory produced soft-paste porcelain in its early years (these pieces are very rare) and began making hard paste after 1783. Royal Copenhagen is perhaps most famous for the massive service made for the Russian Empress Catherine the Great c.1780–1805. Known as Flora Danica, each piece was adorned with a different botanical study, and the pattern is still produced today. Among Royal Copenhagen's other successes are Art Nouveau-style pieces produced in pale grey shades, small figures in regional costumes and animals. The second most famous Danish factory is that of Bing & Grøndahl; founded in 1853, this company produced high-quality wares in similar styles to Royal Copenhagen.

Porcelain was also produced in various centres in the Low Countries. In Belgium the most famous centre was at Tournai; in the Netherlands Amstel, Weesp and Oude Loosdrecht all produced porcelain from 1757–1820. In general although wares from these factories are easily available in their native countries comparatively few examples are seen for sale on the international market.

▲ **OTHER PATTERNS**
Royal Copenhagen also produced a wide range of tablewares in styles derived from Meissen and other European centres, and its more recent products are still available for modest sums. This conventional service, made in the early 20th century and based on French Rococo patterns, contains over 125 pieces including: tureens; platters; sauceboats; leaf-shaped dishes; serving, dinner, dessert and hors d'oeuvres plates; salt, pepper and mustard pots; butter dishes; bowls; cups and saucers; jugs and many more items. Perhaps surprisingly it would be cheaper to buy than a modern equivalent. $4,500–7,500

▲ FLORA DANICA

Versions of this exquisitely painted service have been produced ever since the first one was made (late 18th century) for Catherine the Great. Modern services are less valuable than those made pre-1900. Early painted decoration looks lively and robust; modern decoration may seem flatter. The porcelain on modern versions is finer and more glassy in appearance. This service made c.1900 contains 55 pieces. $21,000–24,000

► FIGURES

Royal Copenhagen figures have enjoyed huge popularity with collectors and are among the most popular pieces. Groups such as this in historical dress provided a favourite theme, as did figures in regional dress. These 20th-century groups of elegant couples are typically well modelled and painted in detail with subtle shades.
$300–450 each

◄ TOURNAI

Figures were one of the specialities of the Belgian Tournai factory, which was the largest manufacturer of porcelain in the Low Countries. Many figures were unglazed and these, made c.1765 and part of a group depicting the Four Seasons, are also typical in their idyllic pastoral theme. They are probably based on a Boucher subject and are easily confused with Sèvres biscuit groups and later Derby wares. $2,750–3,750

OTHER PORCELAIN CENTRES – RUSSIA

Russia's foremost factory was established in St Petersburg c.1748 and became the Imperial Porcelain Factory in 1763. Early wares reflected the style of Meissen but under imperial patronage the factory began making more ambitious pieces. Wares of the early 19th century are particularly distinctive, and characteristically have detailed pictorial decoration and extravagant gilding. After the 1917 Revolution the factory was taken over by the State and went on to produce some interesting Constructivist designs which are much sought after. The factory is still in production. Russia's second most famous factory was established by Francis Gardner in 1776 and flourished until the 1880s when it was taken over by the rival Kuznetsov factory. Gardner was famed for figures in regional costumes and often used matt unglazed surfaces in sombre colours, especially Prussian blue.

► **KUZNETSOV PORCELAIN**

The Kuznetsov factory became Russia's biggest porcelain manufacturer at the turn of the 19th century, producing a wide range of wares for the home and export market. This Kuznetsov beaker (c.1900) is decorated with a portrait of the Tsar's son surrounded by typical Russian designs. Similar commemorative beakers were also produced in enamel. $600–900

▲ **ST PETERSBURG**
Painted with a scene showing a military encampment set against a solid blue ground with a formal ribbon border this sucrier (c.1780) reflects the early Neo-classical fashions popular in England, France and Austria. $1,050–1,350

► **TOPOGRAPHICAL SUBJECTS**
The scene of St Petersburg which decorates the centre of this Imperial Porcelain Factory plate (c.1820) is typically detailed and pictorial. The elaborately moulded rim is however unusual at this time and the gilded wreath decoration is unique to St Petersburg. $1,500–2,250

VALUE

THIS PLATE REFLECTS THE EARLY 19TH-CENTURY FASHION FOR LAVISH GILDING AND DETAILED DECORATION, AND IT HAS SEVERAL ADDITIONAL DESIRABLE FEATURES WHICH ADD SIGNIFICANTLY TO ITS VALUE.
$4,500–7,500

A signature by a leading artist – S. Daladugin.

The soldiers' regiment, rank and the date are also inscribed on the reverse of the plate.

Exceptionally high-quality painting. Similar pieces were made in Meissen and Berlin and often identification relies on marks and differences in the palette.

MARKS

St Petersburg porcelain is marked with a crown and also with the initials of the emperor or empress of that particular period in Roman letters. Other factories often used Cyrillic letters and marks can be the cause of confusion.

◀ POST-REVOLUTIONARY DESIGNS
Porcelain made after the 1917 Revolution was decorated with interesting and innovative angular designs which were inspired by the new styles developed by Russia's Constructivist designers. Subject matter typically reflected the country's new political ideals, and this cup and saucer designed by Maria V. Lebedeva in 1923 is decorated with factory scenes and workers in a typical Constructivist palette of various reds, black and grey.
$2,750–3,000

England did not begin to produce porcelain until the 1740s when the earliest factories were opened at Chelsea, Bow and Bristol. Other important factories that were founded in the 18th century include Derby, Worcester, Longton Hall and Lowestoft. With few exceptions all these early factories produced soft-paste porcelain and most made luxury items as well as domestic wares. Porcelain making was, however, an expensive and precarious business and by the end of the 18th century most of the famous early factories had closed or had been amalgamated with rivals. Among the most successful and long-lived centres of production were Worcester and Derby where factories continued to produce porcelain throughout the 19th and 20th centuries. Industrial development in England in the 19th century led to the establishment of large factories producing a wide variety of goods, ranging from luxury bone china to domestic pottery.

So diverse are the wares produced by major factories such as Worcester, Minton, Spode and Derby that collectors often concentrate on buying ceramics of a particular type rather than choosing from the whole spectrum of products. English porcelain in general offers a rich and varied hunting ground for collectors. The most valuable pieces tend to be those from the 18th century, or larger elaborately decorated pieces made in the 19th century. However, it is still possible to buy some of the smaller 18th-century pieces which are in less than perfect condition for relatively low sums.

BOW

Arguably the earliest of the English porcelain factories Bow, founded in 1744, was called "New Canton" and in its heyday employed hundreds of workmen producing wares for a wide market. Until its closure in 1775, Bow continued to produce huge quantities of blue and white porcelain in the Chinese style, Japanese-inspired coloured wares and a range of figures based on those of Meissen. Slight imperfections in the glaze are characteristic of many pieces. Bow's extensive output means that there is plenty available for collectors to purchase and values tend to be lower than for Chelsea. Prices range from around $225 for tablewares to $7,500 or more for elaborate pieces. Generally most pieces fall within the $1,500–4,500 price range.

▲ **FIGURES**
This model of the actress Kitty Clive in a Garrick farce (c.1750) is simply modelled – a feature associated with early Bow figures. The warm glaze and slight discoloration are also typical. Theatrical subjects have a keen following, and this is early, hence the high price. $6,000–9,000

▶ **DECORATION**

This pair of bottles made c.1755 juxtaposes a Chinese shape with decoration in red, blue and yellow in the style of Japanese Kakiemon, although the flowers and birds are rather more stiffly painted. The peppering on the neck is often seen on Bow porcelain. Identical patterns with exotic long-tailed birds were also found on Chelsea and Arita porcelain (from Japan). $2,250–3,000

◀▶ **IDENTIFICATION**

One of the many domestic blue and white wares produced by Bow, this tankard (c.1760) has a handle finished with a heart-shaped terminal – a charming feature unique to Bow. The rusty discoloration on the base is found on both Bow and Lowestoft porcelain. $1,200–1,500

▶ **LATER FIGURES**

Later Bow figures are identifiable by the tall raised Rococo scroll bases and extensive *bocage* (leafy encrustations). Other factories made similar figures to this but Bow bases are very distinctive. Figures such as this made c.1770 are often marked on the reverse of the tree support. $900–1,350

MARKS
Various incised marks were used but wares are often unmarked. The most common mark on figures is a red anchor and dagger.

CHELSEA

One of the earliest and most important porce-lain factories of its day, the Chelsea factory was founded in c.1745 by Nicholas Sprimont, a French Huguenot silversmith. Chelsea catered for the luxury London market and many of its inventive pieces reflect fashionable silver shapes. Chelsea porcelain is dated and classified according to the various marks used, and among the most sought-after pieces are those of the Red Anchor period, such as the "Hans Sloane" wares decorated with botanical specimens. The factory was taken over by the Derby Porcelain Works in 1769 and finally closed in 1784. Chelsea has a huge following and pieces copied from Meissen at Chelsea can fetch more than the originals.

CHELSEA PORCELAIN

Marks	Characteristics	Dates
Incised triangle	Small, often white pieces, silver shapes	1745–49
Raised anchor	Small, Meissen style, slightly opaque glaze	1749–52
Red anchor	Highly refined, Meissen and Kakiemon styles	1752–57
Gold anchor	Sumptuous decoration, Sèvres style	1759–69

GIRL IN A SWING

A second factory in London made very similar porcelain, especially tiny novelties. Known after its most famous figure, the "Girl in a Swing" it has now been identified as Charles Gouyn's factory in St. James (c.1749–59).

▲ **RAISED ANCHOR**
Jugs have more cachet than teabowls and hence always command a premium. This peach-shaped cream jug from the Raised Anchor period reveals the influence of Meissen in the floral decoration, which is based on the *deutsche Blumen* (German flower) designs but the painting is softer and the handle very naive. $7,500–10,500

▶ **FIGURES**
The British Ambassador in Saxony borrowed numerous Meissen figure models for Chelsea to copy and many figures were copied but the limitations of soft paste meant that the dramatic Meissen poses were impossible to achieve. This Oriental figure (c.1754) is typically softly modelled but columnar in form. $3,750–5,250

► **RED ANCHOR**
The body of Chelsea porcelain is rarely without imperfections and some of the insects and floral sprays decorating the surface of this lobed dish made c.1750–52 probably serve to disguise small blemishes. Chelsea

Red Anchor porcelain is typically greenish in hue. The underside of dishes such as this will have three small raised spur marks – caused by the way the plates were stacked in the kiln during firing. $6,000–9,000

◄ **LATER FIGURES**
Chelsea figures of the later 18th century became more elaborate and usually stood on bases which were richly applied with

floral *bocages* (leafy encrustations). The costumes of figures are usually heavily decorated too and pastel colours are favoured. $3,000–4,500

► **DECORATION**
In the mid-18th century Chelsea turned to the more florid Sèvres style and this pair of vases (c.1765) are typically decorated

with a deep blue ground. Claret grounds were also popular at this time, and the glaze is often patchy, a fault camouflaged by the gilding. $7,500–9,000

DERBY

The Derby factory was founded in 1750 and was known in its early days as "new Dresden" because its particular speciality was producing figures in the style of Meissen. Judging by what has survived, Derby always aimed for the upper echelons of the ceramics market and few early domestic tewares survive; most pieces are elaborate and would have been expensive even when made. The factory is also well known for its decorative vases and other ornamental pieces. Early wares are of very high quality and tend to attract the highest prices. Later pieces are often less detailed but still highly decorative and tend to be more modestly priced. Derby's huge variety of figures reflect different styles, ranging from elaborately sculpted Rococo subjects to simply modelled Neo-classical figures.

▼ WARES
Few wares survive from Derby's early years because the paste used had a tendency to split, so pieces such as this coffee pot (c.1760) are rare. The slightly heavy shape has a distinctive lobed base – a typical Derby feature. $1,800–2,250

▲ EARLY FIGURES
Derby's earliest figures are known as "dry-edge" figures because of the characteristic dry appearance of the edge of the base; many of these pieces were made in the white. Crisp, fine modelling, as demonstrated by this pair of sheep (c.1755), is also a feature of most early figures. White pieces are nearly always less valuable than similar enamelled ones so these would be worth $1,800–2,700.

MARKS
Various marks were used in the early 1750–70 period. After 1770, the factory merged with Chelsea, and marking became more consistent – usually crowned Ds or crossed batons.

◄ **CLASSICAL FIGURES**
This figure of Lord Camden is in the Neo-classical style that by c.1775 had become the height of fashion. The figure is one of a series – Milton, Shakespeare and other national figures were also made. The plain square base is in keeping with the taste for classic simplicity. $1,500–2,250

DERBY & CHELSEA
Derby took over the Chelsea concern in 1769 and for a period it is very difficult to distinguish the products of the two firms since similar models were used and the pastes can be very similar.

► **FRILL VASES**
This so-called "frill vase" (c.1765) has pierced sides and was meant for holding pot pourri. The form was also made by other factories, and Samson produced copies in the 19th century. The large applied flowers are typical of Derby – Chelsea flowers would be more delicate. On pieces of this elaborate nature always check carefully for signs of damage. $1,200–1,800

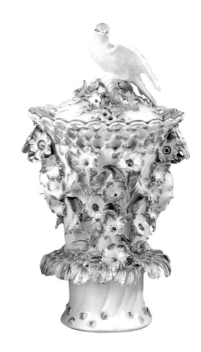

◄ **LATER FIGURES**
In contrast to the stiffer style of Classical figures, these late 18th-century Classical subjects are treated in Rococo style, with elaborate pierced bases. They were meant for vitrines (display cases) so unlike earlier examples which were made to be viewed in the round, the backs would be far less detailed or left entirely plain. $1,050–1,500 for the pair

WORCESTER

The Worcester factory was one of the most successful porcelain manufacturers of the 18th century and is famous, primarily, for the vast amount of tea and coffee wares it produced. Together with Chelsea, Worcester remains perhaps the most popular of the 18th-century factories with collectors. The porcelain made by Worcester contained soapstone which made it very stable and able to withstand boiling water. As a result vast quantities of hollowwares have survived and so daunting is the enormous range available that collectors often concentrate their efforts on a particular area such as early wares, transfer printed designs, teapots or coffee cups. Prices for Worcester pieces are generally lower than for Chelsea ones. Among the most readily available and collectable printed patterns are the Three Flowers pattern, Fence Pattern and Fisherman and Cormorant pattern.

CLASSIFICATION
Worcester is classified according to the factory's owners:
- Dr Wall or First period 1751–74
- Davis period 1774–83
- Flight period 1783–92
- Flight & Barr period 1792–1804
- Barr, Flight & Barr period 1804–13
- Flight, Barr & Barr period 1813–40
- Chamberlain & Co. 1840–52
- Kerr & Binns period 1852–62
- Worcester Royal Porcelain Co Ltd from 1862 (see p124)

MARKS
The usual Worcester mark is an open crescent, either painted or printed. The factory also marked with a square Chinese fret with cross hatching and used pseudo-Chinese or alchemical marks.

▲ EARLY TRANSFER PRINTING
Worcester started using underglaze transfer printing from c.1757. Printed wares, such as this double-handled pierced basket (c.1770), tend to be less expensive than hand-painted pieces of a similar date but are still keenly collected. $600–900

▼ CHINOISERIE
Early wares were heavily inspired by Chinese decoration and this sauce boat (c.1755) is typically painted with a fanciful Chinese landscape. The body has a bluish tone that is a feature of much early Worcester. $1,200–1,800

◀ DECORATION

Floral patterns inspired by Oriental designs were the most popular form of hand-painted design on 18th-century Worcester. This fluted coffee cup and saucer are typically painted in *gros bleu* panels separated by bunches of flowers. Elsewhere in England the Japanese style had long faded from favour but Worcester produced Japanese-inspired designs well into the 1770s when this was made. $600–900

▶ COLOURED GROUNDS

Coloured grounds, as seen on this covered vase, were popular in the 1760s–80s but had a tendency to blotchiness. This problem was often overcome by using a blue ground printed with an overlapping fish scale pattern. Yellow, green and claret grounds were also used sometimes. $3,750–5,250

▼ CHAMBERLAINS WORCESTER

Chamberlains Worcester was a rival factory which produced wares in similar styles. The factory eventually amalgamated with Flight, Barr & Barr to become Chamberlain & Co in 1840. Pieces are usually marked "Chamberlains Worcester". This Chamberlain vase (c.1815) is painted with feathers, a much sought after subject. $3,750–5,250

◀ FLIGHT, BARR & BARR

Lavish gilding and exquisitely detailed painted decoration are hallmarks of Worcester porcelain of the early 19th century. This campana-shaped vase (c.1820), one of a pair, reflects the prevailing fashion for Neo-classical forms and is decorated with minutely observed botanical subjects. $3,000–4,500 for a pair

OTHER ENGLISH FACTORIES

In general most minor 18th-century English porcelain factories produced useful wares, such as tea and coffee wares and dinner services, rather than purely decorative items. Blue and white was the most popular form of decoration, but some factories also used a polychrome palette based loosely on the *famille rose* of Chinese porcelain. Of the minor factories, Limehouse was the first to be established in 1745 (until 1748), followed by Vauxhall in 1751 (until 1764), Lowestoft 1757 (until 1799) and Caughley (c.1775–99). In Liverpool several factories were established; among the most important were Richard Chaffers (1754/5–65), Samuel Gilbody (1754–61), Phillip Christian (1765–78) and Seth Pennington (1778–99). Although wares by these small manufacturers are less readily available than those by larger establishments such as Chelsea and Worcester, all are popular with collectors. Recently discovered factories such as Vauxhall and Limehouse have a particularly keen following and command a premium. Caughley, the most prolific of the minor English factories, tends to be less sought after and the factory also produced printed wares which are less valuable than some of its hand-decorated pieces.

▼ **LONGTON HALL**
Moulded patterns using floral and vegetable motifs were a particular speciality of the Longton Hall factory and this strawberry leaf plate, made c.1755, is typical of the factory's output. The body is similar to Chelsea Red Anchor porcelain and there are often flaws in the glaze. $900–1,200

LONGTON HALL WARES

Blue and white tablewares, copies of Chinese *famille rose* designs, tureens and pot pourri vases are among the varied output.

▲ **CAUGHLEY**
A dense chinoiserie pattern is printed on this part-tea set (c.1790), a typical decorative technique for this factory. The use of gilding is also characteristic of Caughley. This is part of a set which originally would have had tea bowls, a pot stand and possibly a spoon tray too. Caughley porcelain is made using soaprock and may have a greyish tinge. $225–300 for 6 pieces

▶ LIVERPOOL

This helmet-shaped sauce boat (1765–76) is attributed to Phillip Christian's factory, which produced cream jugs, sauce boats and a variety of tea and coffee wares. The decoration here is slightly awkward and the painting has overshot the moulded cartouche. The ribbed foot is seen on wares from other Liverpool factories. $750–1,050

◀ LOWESTOFT FIGURES

In general the Lowestoft factory tended to produce very few figures but dogs were more common than other subjects. These examples (1760–70) are inspired by Meissen originals. Lowestoft used a phosphatic body for its figures which often has a slightly greenish tinge. Over time, unfortunately, it suffers from brown rust-like discoloration. $3,000–4,500 each

MARKS

- **Caughley** marked with a "C" (similar to Worcester), or the word "Salopian" or "S"
- **Longton Hall** no marks used
- **Vauxhall** spurious Chinese marks are very occasionally found
- **Lowestoft** crossed swords; a crescent similar to Worcester is also used sometimes

◀ VAUXHALL

Vauxhall is a recently discovered factory. These bottle vases (1755) are very similar to Worcester wares but are more vibrantly coloured. Vases of this shape were particularly popular in London and were also made by the Bow factory. The shape has sagged slightly in firing, a defect characteristic of this factory. $12,000–18,000 for a pair

ROYAL CROWN DERBY

Two different factories flourished in Derby in the later part of the 19th century. The most important was the Derby Crown Porcelain Co Ltd, later to become Royal Crown Derby; second came the Derby King Street factory, headed by Samson Hancock. The two factories were rivals and made similar pieces mainly based on patterns and shapes made in Derby earlier in the century, which in turn were based on designs by Sèvres with coloured grounds and raised gilding. Imari wares were another particular Derby speciality and reached a peak of perfection in the 1890s–1915. After World War I production deteriorated and later pieces from the two factories are far less sought after today. Traditionally considered the poor relation of Worcester and Minton, Derby produced wares which were undervalued until relatively recently. Prices have escalated dramatically over the last few years, particularly for fine cabinet pieces with signed decoration.

◀ DECORATION

Derby porcelain is famed for its high-quality decoration and the finest Derby pieces made after 1895 were signed by the artist. This plate, made for the Duke of York's marriage in 1893, is by Derby's most famous decorator Désiré Leroy. He was a French decorator who had worked at Sèvres and was famed for his painting and gilding. $3,750–4,500

DECORATORS

Pieces by leading decorators are much sought after. Among the names to look out for are:
- **William Dean** a specialist in yachts and ships
- **Désiré Leroy** the best-known of all Derby painters, who trained at Sèvres
- **Cuthbert Gresley** and **Albert Gregory** well-known flower painters (see p123).

IMARI

One of Royal Crown Derby's most successful specialities was a range of Imari-style patterns. Each pattern has its own name; this toy saucepan (c.1910) is decorated in one of the most popular patterns, the Old Witches'. Cigar pattern and King's pattern are also popular. $350–400 Miniature pieces, such as this saucepan, are among the most valuable of all Imari wares. Rare shapes, such as milk churns, flat irons and casseroles, can fetch $750–1,200 each.

▲ FLOWER PAINTERS
This deep blue ground vase made in 1913 is typically based on 18th-century Sèvres porcelain styles; the central panel is filled with a bouquet of roses and other flowers, skillfully painted by Albert Gregory, one of the most famous flower painters at Derby. Cuthbert Gresley is also famed for his floral subjects. $1,200–1,500

▼ FIGURES
A wide range of popular figures, many of which were originally made in the 18th century, were produced by the King Street factory. This traditional model of the Tailor on a Goat was reissued c.1900, and is marked "SH" for Samson Hancock. $225–300

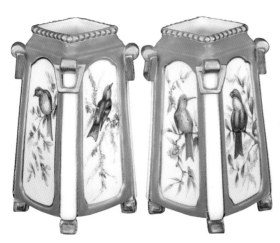

▲ CONDITION
One of these vases (made c.1880 by the Derby Crown Porcelain Co) was cracked and the gilding was slightly worn. In better condition they might fetch twice as much. $375–525

MARKS
Derby pieces are nearly always clearly marked, usually in red, with a printed crown and cipher and normally a year code; these marks are rarely faked. The King Street factory used the original Derby painted mark with the initials "SH" on each side. Sometimes these initials have been ground away in an attempt to make the piece look older than it really is.

ROYAL WORCESTER

The Worcester Royal Porcelain Company was formed in 1862; the kaleidoscopic range of wares produced by this factory spanned from humble domestic goods to the finest cabinet pieces exquisitely decorated by leading painters. Royal Worcester's extraordinary commercial success was largely due to the inspired direction of the factory's artistic director, R. W. Binns, who kept his finger on the pulse of changing fashion and was able to cater to public demand. Worcester excelled in designs of Eastern inspiration; as Japanese art infiltrated the Western world the factory began producing patterns inspired by Japanese

ceramics and Indian ivories, Persian ceramics and Oriental metalwork. Worcester is also famed for unusual finishes such as "blush ivory", an effect which was much copied in Germany and Austria. Among the most sought-after pieces of Royal Worcester are signed pieces by leading names such as the Stinton family, Charley Baldwyn and Harry Davis. Figures by Worcester's leading modeller James Hadley are also keenly collected, as are those made in the 20th century by Freda Doughty. Worcester also produced a series of limited-edition figures; these have not held their value as well as figures by Doulton.

◀ DECORATION
Japanese-inspired design was a popular form of decoration on many Royal Worcester pieces; this 1872 vase with frogs, one of a pair, is an amusing example copied exactly from an Oriental prototype. $3,000–3,750 pair

▶ JAMES HADLEY
Hadley was Royal Worcester's most famous modeller. Working in the 19th century, he was responsible for a series of blush ivory figures such as this "piping boy" (1889) which remain particularly popular with collectors today. Value depends on the rarity of the figure; this example would be worth $900–1,050.

▲ THE STINTONS
Harry and his father John Stinton specialized in painting Highland cattle in mountains. James, John's brother, painted game birds rather than cattle. Pieces such as this vase by Harry Stinton, made in 1919, are very popular but value varies greatly according to size. This measures 8in (21cm) high and would be worth $1,500–2,100

▼ **FREDA DOUGHTY**
Freda Doughty, one of the most popular Worcester modellers working in the 1930s, produced a series of children at play, such as this figure known as "Dancing Waves". Royal Worcester also produced animal models by Doris Lindner. $250–300

▲ **IVORY DECORATION**
The "blush ivory" finish provided a background for formal floral decoration which proved to be very popular in the late 19th/early 20th century. It is seen to great effect on this *pot pourri* vase. Many other makers both in England and abroad copied this unusal Royal Worcester colouring. $375–525

▶ **VALUE**
Most blush ivory vases such as this one (c.1910) were decorated by hand, applying colour to a black printed etched outline of the design. The best designs are by Edward Raby who sometimes signed his work with his initials somewhere in the printed design. The blush ivory ground was sometimes painted entirely by hand and this adds to value. $375–450

MARKS
Standard Royal Worcester marks are date-coded with a series of letters and dots. By looking in a specialist mark book you can work out the year of manufacture.

• From 1862 "Worcester Royal Porcelain Works", within a circle surmounted by a crown enclosing a cipher and crescent with the date code beneath were used.

• After 1891 "Royal Worcester England" was used (as above).

• From 1938 the words "Bone China" appear in addition to the standard mark.

NANTGARW & SWANSEA

The fortunes of Wales' two most famous porcelain factories were inextricably linked. William Billingsley, England's foremost flower painter on porcelain, opened the Nantgarw works in 1813, and shortly after moved to the Cambrian pottery, Swansea, where true porcelain had not hitherto been produced. A few years later he returned to Nantgarw, but such large quantities of porcelain were lost in firing that the company was soon in financial distress and closed down four years later. Billingsley is famed for producing fine white highly translucent porcelain of unrivalled quality and products were aimed at the upper echelons of the London market. Many pieces were sold in the white and decorated in London. Not surprisingly, considering its short-lived existence, Welsh porcelain is scarcer than that from other factories – and for this reason commands a premium. Many unmarked pieces are misascribed and identification is a matter of expert opinion. Pieces painted in Wales are more sought after than those decorated elsewhere – the most famous decorators were Thomas Baxter, Thomas Pardoe, David Evans and William Pollard as well as Billingsley himself.

▶ **DECORATION**
Decoration on much Welsh porcelain was inspired by French taste of the late Regency period, with neo-Rococo flowers on a white ground a typical form. This Swansea plate (c.1815) is typically decorated with delicately painted flowers on a white ground. $750–1,050

◀ **LONDON DECORATED WARES**
Although as a general rule pieces decorated in London tend to be less valuable than those decorated in Wales, decorative examples such as this made c.1820 with its detailed bird border are still popular with collectors. $1,050–1,500

BODY

On Swansea porcelain the body may be one of three different types and this can affect value. Early pieces were made from "glassy" paste; the most sought-after pieces are made from "duck egg" paste – with a slight greyish tinge; later pieces were made from what is known as "trident" paste and are considered somewhat less desirable.

▼ WARES

Nantgarw mainly produced plates, cups, saucers and a range of small ornaments. Swansea was famed for tea and dessert services, cabinet pieces and decorative objects such as taper sticks and inkwells. This tureen, made c.1815, is unmarked but the roses and shape are characteristic of Swansea. $750–900

◀ NANTGARW

Beautifully painted floral subjects were produced at both Nantgarw and Swansea and the marks are often the only way to tell the two apart. This Nantgarw plate (c.1817–20), stylistically very similar to the one opposite, is typically painted with a bouquet of irises, tulips and other flowers. $750–1,050

MARKS

Nantgarw wares were usually marked with an impressed "NANTGARW CW" (for china works). Many Swansea pieces were marked in red with a painted, stencilled or impressed "SWANSEA" .

NANT-GARW
C.W.

BEWARE

Many French porcelain blanks, especially vases, were also decorated in London with identical decoration to that used on Welsh plates. Fake Swansea marks are also known to have been added to English porcelain to make it more valuable.

MINTON

The Minton factory, founded by Thomas Minton in 1798, was one of the 19th century's biggest and most varied producers of every type of ceramic, ranging from architectural fittings such as tiles and majolica, to humble earthenware and fine bone china. Minton's greatest period spans from the mid- to late 19th century, although the company is still in production today. Among its finest wares were pieces made using the *pâte sur pâte* technique, which had been developed on the Continent. *Pâte sur pâte* was introduced to Minton, and the English market, by Marc-Louis Solon, a former employee of Sèvres. Japanese styles also influenced the factory c.1870–80; many

patterns were based on Japanese porcelain, including cloisonné, using brilliant turquoise enamels. The Art Nouveau style was reflected in Secessionist wares designed for Minton by John Wadsworth and Leon Solon. Prices for Minton not surprisingly reflect the variety of objects made by the factory. Top examples of the sophisticated *pâte sur pâte* technique were expensive when made and similarly rank among the factory's most valuable products today; even plates cost around $1,500. Printed tiles designed by leading artists such as John Moyr Smith can be bought for $37, however, and many other less elaborate pieces can be found for similarly modest sums.

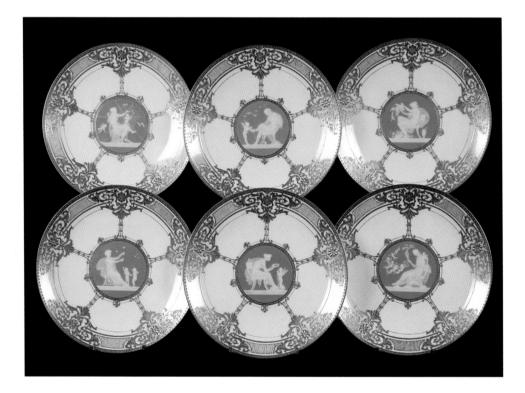

▲ *PÂTE SUR PÂTE*

Pâte sur pâte was one of Minton's most sophisticated and expensive products. The technique involved building up decorative cameos by

applying layers of white slip to a darker base. Many of these pieces were also adorned with lavish raised gilding. These plates (1911) are by Alboin Birks, one of the finest

exponents of the technique. Vases from the Minton factory decorated using the *pâte sur pâte* technique are also highly sought after by collectors. $1,500–2,100 each

▲ SERVICES

As well as ornamental pieces Minton also produced dinner, dessert and tea services, many of which are still available at very reasonable prices. These plates, from an eight-piece part-dessert service date-marked 1870, are decorated with rich turquoise borders and sprays of wild flowers. $225–300 for the part-set

▲ ORIENTAL DECORATION

Japanese cloisonné provided the inspiration behind a range of brilliantly decorated ornamental pieces such as this vase (c.1876) in which gilding was used to simulate the effect of the copper wires used in true cloisonné to divide the panels of differently coloured enamels. Pieces similar to this were designed by Dr Christopher Dresser but this example is unsigned. $525–750

► SECESSIONIST STYLE

Minton was highly original in its use of innovative design in the late 19th century. Its "Secessionist" wares are identifiable by their unusual shapes and simple decoration. This vase is probably by John Wadsworth, a leading designer of the day; it is decorated using a slip-trailed technique and reflects the influence of continental Art Nouveau. Another leading designer in this style was Marc-Louis Solon. $300–450

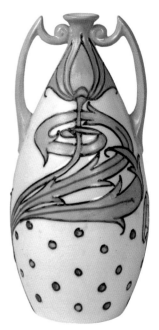

MARKS

Nearly all Minton is marked, either with the name "MINTON" or "MINTONS". Pieces made before c.1914 usually have an additional date code mark.

COALPORT

Founded in the last decade of the 18th century the Coalport factory made fine ornamental wares alongside domestic pieces such as tea and dinner services, and the factory is still in production today. The varied tastes of the day are mirrored in the changing styles of the factory's output. Coalport mimicked styles first made by Meissen, Dresden and Sèvres with coloured grounds, eccentric shapes and generous helpings of decoration. The factory is also famous for flower-encrusted pieces made in the 1830s; these were known as "Coalbrookdale" but were in fact produced by the same company. Confusingly for collectors Coalport was also a major supplier of white porcelain to independent china painters and many wares carry decoration which was not done at the Coalport factory.

◀ "COALBROOKDALE"
Elaborate floral decoration and scrolls were hallmarks of the "English Dresden style" fashionable in the 1830s. Pieces in this style made at Coalport are popularly known as "Coalbrookdale"; this typical clock case is lavishly decorated in the Rococo style. $1,200–1,800

▼ JEWELLED COALPORT
At the turn of the century until the 1920s the Coalport works achieved huge success with jewelled porcelain, a distinctive decorative technique made by placing beads of turquoise enamel on a gilded or coloured ground. These pieces are much collected and even tiny cups and saucers can cost $600–750 or more.

▲ DECORATORS
Coalport allowed artists to sign pieces in the late 19th and 20th centuries. Among the best-known decorators are Edward Ball and Percy Simpson who painted landscapes. John Randall, a specialist in exotic bird subjects, and Frederick Chivers, a specialist in still life, decorated this elaborate vase (c.1905), one of a pair. $1,500–2,250 for the pair

ROCKINGHAM

Perhaps better known than it deserves to be, this short-lived factory is famous for its rather unconventional output. Founded in Yorkshire in 1826 by the Brameld family, the company took its name and mark from its financial backer, the Earl Fitzwilliam, Marquis of Rockingham. The company concentrated on ambitious decoration and in 1830 began making a service for King William IV, which ultimately led to its financial ruin; 12 years later,

in 1842, the firm finally closed. Despite the limited output Rockingham is extremely popular with collectors and pieces command a premium compared with other more prolific factories. Simple cups and saucers fetch from $150 and more; small vases start at around $750–1,200. Most Rockingham was marked but many unmarked pieces by Minton and Coalport have been wrongly attributed over the years to Rockingham.

◄ QUALITY

Lavish gilding and accomplished painted decoration are typical of Rockingham. This plate is of particularly fine quality since it was a specimen design for the celebrated service produced by the factory for the coronation of William IV and first used for Queen Victoria's coronation.
$4,500–7,500

► ANIMALS

Rockingham produced an assortment of animals including cats, dogs and rabbits. Rockingham animals, are invariably marked unlike those of other factories. This cat was made c.1830.
$1,200–1,500

▲ PLAQUES

Plaques are rare among Rockingham's output and this example is particularly unusual and valuable because it is signed and dated by Thomas Steel, a leading artist who is known to have worked at the firm in 1830.
$6,000–7,500

MARKS

A griffin taken from Earl Fitzwilliam's arms was first printed in red, then purple after c.1830 when "Manufacturer to the King" was added.

Rockingham Works Brameld

SPODE

This large Staffordshire factory was founded by Josiah Spode in 1776, and from the end of the 18th century throughout the 19th century produced a vast range of domestic earthenwares and Parian, as well as grander bone china services and ornamental pieces reflecting the prevailing taste for Classical or Rococo style (see p78 and p134). The company was bought out by Copeland & Garrett in 1833 and is still in production. Spode's most distinctive products include the Imari patterns popular c.1815–25; pieces with coloured grounds; and pieces with hand-painted decoration by leading decorators such as C. F. Hürten. Lavish gilding is also a feature of many of the best pieces. This is a vast and diverse collecting field and although less distinctive than those of some other factories, products range from highly elaborate ornamental wares to humbler bat-printed wares.

MARKS   **SPODE**

Before 1830 Spode usually hand-painted this name on porcelain (or impressed on pottery). After 1833 the names "Copeland & Garrett" usually appear with "Late Spode" in the middle. The word "Copeland" is used alone after 1847.

◀ **PRINTED WARES**
Among the least expensive Spode pieces are bat-printed wares such as this milk jug of c.1815, which is decorated with a picturesque landscape. Bat printing was a method that relied on soft glue rather than paper to transfer printed designs.
$135–180

▶ **PATTERNS**
Patterns are identified by numbers and this vase (c.1825), decorated in a floral design on a blue and gilt scale ground, is an example of pattern number 1166, one of the most popular of all Spode patterns with today's collectors.
$750–1,200

◀ **DECORATORS**
Decorators at Spode did not usually sign their work; their names are not generally known but their high-quality decoration can attract high prices none the less. This straight-sided chocolate cup and stand (c.1815) is skilfully painted with loose sprays of flowers within rectangular gilt panels but the low value reflects the damage it has suffered.
$300–450

DAVENPORT

Another successful Staffordshire factory, Davenport was established in 1794 by John Davenport and produced earthenware, basalt, creamware, bone china and even glass throughout the 19th century, until its closure in 1887. Davenport has no particularly distinctive style but is recognized for decoration of high quality. Pieces were usually marked with name and pattern number which, along with their style, are helpful clues for dating.

Davenport patented a technique for making thinly potted porcelain plaques, many of which were sold to independent decorators. Although popular with collectors, Davenport tends to fetch lower prices than pieces by Worcester, Swansea or Rockingham, even though it is often of equally fine quality and can provide excellent value. Among the most affordable pieces to look out for are blue and white printed plates from $45–105.

◀ **DECORATION**
This is an early Davenport plate (c.1810–15), heavily decorated with chinoiserie inspired by

Meissen. The highly detailed form of decoration seen here is unique to the Davenport factory.
$210–270

MARKS
Davenport was marked with a crown between c.1870 and 1886; the words "Davenport Longport" also appear in some early and later marks.

SERVICES
Davenport produced some very extensive dinner services using porcelain and various other less expensive materials. This part-

dessert service (c.1815) is made from pearlware; other large services were made from ironstone (see p75). $1,500–2,250 (for 17 pieces, allowing for some damage)

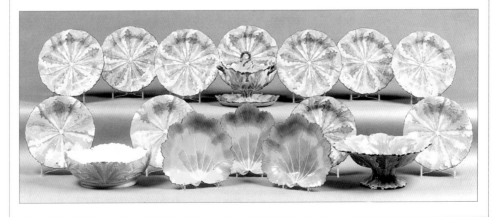

PARIAN

Named after Roman marble quarries at Paros, Parian was a hugely popular 19th-century material used to make inexpensive imitations of marble sculpture. Copeland and Minton both claim to have invented Parian in the 1840s and by the mid-century many other factories were also producing it. Copeland called the substance "statuary porcelain" in the early days, while Wedgwood termed its version "Carrara ware" after another famous Italian marble quarry. Parian's advantage was that it contained a high proportion of glass crystals and its vitreous nature meant that dirt did not adhere to it. Many of the leading 19th-century sculptors designed models to be reproduced in Parian; copies of famous antique works were also made, as well as busts of literary and historical personalities.

◀ MAKERS
Leading factories include Copeland, Wedgwood, Minton and Robinson & Leadbeater, a firm specializing in Parian. This figure of Dorothea was made in enormous numbers c.1865–70 by Minton from a model by the sculptor John Bell.
$525–675

MARKS
Parian figures are usually marked by their maker on the base or on the back of the model. Some pieces may also be titled and have a date code.

VALUE
Value depends on a piece's maker, its decorative appeal and its size. Prices range from under $60 for small busts to over $1,500 for larger subjects.

◀ SUBJECTS
Parian figures depicting famous royal, political and literary figures were also popular. This figure of the Duke of Wellington is by Samuel Alcock & Co after a sculpture by G. Abbott, and dates from 1852.
$525–750

ART UNIONS
Parian figures are often stamped with names such as "The Crystal Palace Union" or "Art Union of London". To raise funds for the Arts, "art unions" ran lotteries where art lovers could buy tickets in the hope that they might win an original work such as a specially commissioned Parian figure. Copeland was one of numerous firms who made figures for art unions.

BELLEEK

Established in 1863 by David McBirney and Robert Williams Armstrong in County Fermanagh, Northern Ireland, Belleek specialized in producing an incredibly thin high-quality white porcelain using a glazed Parian body. Warm and creamy in appearance, Belleek resembled the texture and translucence of sea shells and before long the factory began making wares in the forms of shells decorated with iridescent glaze, as well as finely woven baskets. Belleek has always been popular in the United States, and in fact workers from the Irish factory emigrated and set up rival establishments there; their products are termed "American Belleek". The factory is still in production and the same designs have been produced throughout its existence. Small pieces of Belleek cost from $45 while larger more elaborate pieces such as baskets can fetch between $6,000 and 7,500.

▲ DATING
Baskets can be dated from the number of strands from which the centres are woven. Baskets such as this from the 19th century are three-stranded; after c.1900, as potting became even finer, four strands were used. $375–525 (damaged)

MARKS
The first mark with the word "BELLEEK" in black was used only until 1891 after which the second mark was used, adding the word "IRELAND" to the name. More modern marks are in green or gold.

▲ TEAWARES
Belleek's unusual teawares are also popular with collectors. The value of teasets depends on the number of pieces they have. This delicately green-tinged jug, made in the late 19th early 20th century in the Neptune pattern, is worth $100–120.

▲ DESIGNS
The fine lustrous body perfected at Belleek looked like mother-of-pearl and shells provide a recurring theme for many ornamental pieces. This pair of oval shell jelly dishes (c.1870–90) are moulded with shells among coral branches enriched with pink and turquoise. $225–300

CONDITION
The fineness of Belleek makes it vulnerable to damage and even hairline cracks can devastate value. The basket top left has had some restoration; in perfect condition it might be worth $1,500–3,000.

Twentieth-century pottery and porcelain is without doubt the most rapidly growing collecting area in ceramics. As top examples from the traditional collecting fields of 18th- and 19th-century ceramics have become increasingly rare and expensive, collectors have turned their attentions to more recent manufacturers, and makers such as Carlton, Susie Cooper and Poole now have a very well-established following.

Twentieth-century ceramics encompasses on the one hand pieces by leading commercial designers and illustrious studio potters, and on the other a plethora of commercially produced wares which reflect the prevailing taste of the day. In general large pieces designed or made by well-established designers tend to be visually more striking and therefore attract the highest prices. But for collectors on a limited budget there is a rich hunting ground of smaller designer-made pieces as well as stylish wares by lesser manufacturers which can still be found very affordably. The modern geometric forms that typify Art Deco styles of the 1920s and 1930s are particularly popular with today's collectors, and pieces in characteristically dramatic shapes or with interesting designs will often be worth far more than less stylish pieces by the same designer.

Ornamental figurines, which have been made since the earliest days of ceramics, have continued to be an extremely popular field with collectors and among the most eagerly sought are figures by Doulton, Wade and Beswick which are still readily available for a huge range of prices.

CLARICE CLIFF

Acclaimed as "a poet in pottery" Clarice Cliff was one of the most prolific and innovative of potters working in the 1920s; her brightly coloured wares with streamlined modern shapes have become synonymous with Art Deco style and enjoy huge popularity with collectors. Clarice Cliff was born in Tunstall in 1899 and worked for A. J. Wilkinson, a Staffordshire pottery where she was given free rein to introduce a new range of hand-painted pottery called Hand Painted Bizarre by Clarice Cliff. By 1930 the success of Cliff's designs led to her appointment as art director of the firm, overseeing a hundred decorators and producing a range of designs.

▲ DESIGNS
Clarice Cliff drew on a range of sources as inspiration for her patterns. Floral and foliate patterns include Crocus, Autumn, Alpine, Capri and Latona. Landscape provides the theme for Secrets and textile design inspired Blue Chintz and Appliqué. This lotus-shaped jug features the rare Comet pattern. $4,500–6,000

DESIGNERS TO LOOK OUT FOR
During the 1930s Clarice Cliff commissioned designs from leading artists such as Paul Nash, Duncan Grant, Frank Brangwyn, Dame Laura Knight and Graham Sutherland.

◀ **VALUE**
Value depends on the rarity of the design and the appeal of the form. Modern streamlined shapes are especially desirable, as are unusual patterns and colour variants. This Tennis pattern tea set combines an unusual avant-garde pattern with highly innovative form; hence its high value. $9,000–10,500

▶ **FIGURATIVE PIECES**
Clarice Cliff produced a limited range of cut-out silhouette figures painted on both sides

entitled The Age of Jazz series. This group is formed as a plaque showing two couples dancing the tango. $9,000–10,500

SETS
It is possible to build up sets of Clarice Cliff by buying individual pieces if you choose one of the more common designs, but pieces from rarer styles are more difficult to track down.

◀ **FAKES**
Fakes with photographically copied marks have appeared on the market in the last decade. These are often identifiable by the inferior quality of the painting and by the fact that the marks look fuzzy - the ones on the left are fake, those on the right genuine. $300–900 (for the genuine ones)

MOORCROFT

One of the most successful English ceramicists in the Art Nouveau style, William Moorcroft (1872–1945) was a Staffordshire-born and trained potter who began designing for the firm of Macintyre & Co in 1898. Moorcroft is best known for his use of slip-trailing decorations called Florian ware. Most of his early designs combine Art Nouveau naturalism, in which identifiable flowers, mushrooms or landscapes often form part of the design, with shapes influenced by Eastern and later Classical ceramics. Moorcroft supplied wares to Liberty's who often sold pieces with pewter mounts, and many wares were also sent abroad. In 1913 Moorcroft set up his own factory and new designs were gradually introduced. Moorcroft's son Walter joined the firm in 1935 and also produced mainly floral designs in a distinctive style. Value depends on the rarity of the design and the form. Prices range from $300 to $7,500 or more for unusual colour variants. The factory is still in production today and continues to turn out a range of innovative designs.

◀ FLORIAN WARE
Florian decoration was made by "drawing" on to the pot with thin lines of clay, rather like icing a cake, and then applying colours in between the lines. This oviform vase (c.1903) is decorated in autumnal shades with an Art Nouveau tulip pattern. $7,500–10,500

MARKS
Moorcroft marks vary; "W Moorcroft Des" or "WM des" is often found on Florian from the Macintyre period. Pieces produced in his own factory were usually marked "MOORCROFT BURSLEM", impressed with either "WM" or "W. Moorcroft".

▼ MODERN MOORCROFT
The Moorcroft factory is still in production and some of its limited edition products are set to become collectables of the future. This modern vase was designed in 1988 by Sally Tuffin, in a limited edition of 250 for the Canadian market, and shows a design with polar bears in an Arctic setting created by using the traditional slip-trailing techniques for which Moorcroft is known. $375–525

▶ PERSIAN PATTERN
Inspired by Iznik and Persian ceramics Moorcroft's Persian pattern is slightly more finely detailed than Persian ware by de Morgan (see p85), and is highly decorative and popular with collectors. This two-handled vase (c.1915) is typically decorated with stylized flowers and leaves. $4,500–6,000

WEMYSS WARE

Folksy and charmingly naive, Wemyss ware was first produced in the Fife pottery in south-east Scotland in 1880. The simple wares were decorated with highly distinctive hand-painted motifs of cabbage roses, fruit, birds and farmyard animals and sold through Thomas Goode in London. In 1930 the Scottish factory closed and the moulds were sold to the Bovey Tracey Pottery in Devon, where the same designs continued to be produced until the 1950s and beyond. Prices for Wemyss vary according to the age and rarity of the particular piece. A rare Wemyss cat has recently fetched $16,500, but most pieces sell for between $450 and $900, and you can find small items for under $150.

▶ **DECORATION**
Wemyss' distinctively colourful style of decoration was created using underglaze enamelling. Flowers were a recurring theme and this early 20th-century teapot is adorned with a cheerful buttercup pattern typical of the bold designs for which the Scottish factory is famed. $300–525

◀ **PIGS**
Ornamental pigs, often covered with cabbage roses, are among the best loved of Wemyss wares. Prices vary according to size; this pig made in 1920 is fairly small and would be worth $300–400, but larger pigs can fetch a great deal more.

▼ **COCKEREL PATTERNS**
Many Wemyss designs were by Karel Nekola, a Bohemian artist who worked for Wemyss for many years. This vase (c.1900) is decorated with cockerels and hens – one of Nekola's most popular designs. $600–750

MARKS
- Early Wemyss ware has an impressed mark and the words "Wemyss Ware R H & S" in a semi-circle.
- The single word "Wemyss" was used as a mark throughout the 19th and 20th centuries.
- The words "Thos Goode" usually indicate an early production.
- In 1930 the factory moved to Bovey Tracey in Devon, after this time the words "Made in England" can appear with the Wemyss mark.

COMMEMORATIVE CERAMICS

Commemorative ceramics are a vast collecting area encompassing anything made to mark a particular historical event. Royal weddings and deaths, coronations, jubilees, wars, elections and strikes have all been immortalized in ceramic form and collectors tend to concentrate on a particular theme or character rather than on the subject in general. Any ceramic commemoratives that predate the coronation of Queen Victoria are rare and correspondingly valuable. Most commemoratives date from the mid-19th century onwards, when improved methods of transfer printing allowed potters to make souvenirs inexpensively.

◀ **WILLIAM IV CORONATION**
Transfer prints on early commemorative wares can contain fascinating historical details. This Staffordshire pottery jug (1830) is unusual in showing William at the Coronation ceremony in Westminster Abbey. $400–600

▼ **MAKERS**
In the 20th century vast quantities of royal souvenirs were made. Values remain low unless the piece is unusual or by top manufacturers. This Wedgwood tankard by Richard Guyatt marks the marriage of Princess Anne and Captain Mark Phillips in 1973. $45–75

▲ **VALUE**
Commemoratives of obscure events are less sought after than those celebrating more significant events. Huge numbers of mugs marked the Diamond Jubilee of Queen Victoria in 1897; this mug has more details than most. $90–150

▶ **RECENT COMMEMORATIVES**
Most commemoratives from recent decades are still available for under $10 but cartoon mugs from the wedding of Prince Charles and Lady Diana Spencer are already increasing in value. This mug was designed by Mark Boxer to commemorate the royal wedding in 1981 and has a comical handle shaped as an ear. $45–67

GOSS & CRESTED CHINA

Crested china was made as seaside souvenirs during the late 19th and early 20th centuries when the principal maker was W. H. Goss. Decorated with the coats of arms of the most popular holiday resorts, these pieces provided visitors with souvenirs of their stay and were made in vast quantities until c.1930 when the fashion for Goss abated. Goss pieces were invariably well made and although the Arcadian and Carlton works in England and other factories in Germany made similar crested pieces none could rival Goss for quality. The most sought-after pieces are "Goss cottages" which can fetch upwards of $300.

▶ **COTTAGES**
Goss buildings, representing the homes of national heroes such as Anne Hathaway's cottage (seen here), Lloyd George's home or Charles Dickens' house or other landmarks, can form the theme of a fascinating collection and have become extremely popular. $45–60

◀ **FIGURES**
Apart from heraldic ceramics and model buildings Goss also produced a keenly collected range of decorative figures, some based on famous sculptures such as this late 19th-century bust depicting "The Veiled Bride". $700–1,050

MARKS
- Genuine Goss china should have a printed mark with a hawk.
- Some crested pieces which were produced in Germany are marked "GEMMA".
- Beware of fake cottages produced with spurious hand-painted Goss marks.

WHAT TO LOOK FOR
World War I pieces from Barmouth, decorated with the flags of Britain's allies, are among the more desirable examples of crested china wares you are likely to come across. Other sought-after pieces include:
- figures
- lighthouses (and other buildings)
- animals.

SUSIE COOPER

Born in 1902, Susan Vera Cooper became one of the most influential ceramic designers of her generation, producing a wide range of commercial wares in a distinctively subtle style. After working for a while for A. E. Gray, Susie Cooper set up her own company in 1929. Early output mainly concentrated on earthenwares, often hand-painted; fine bone china began to be produced after the Second World War. In 1961 the firm of Susie Cooper merged with R. H. & S. L. Plant which in turn was taken over by Wedgwood in 1966. Wedgwood reissued some of Susie Cooper's early designs such as Pink Fern, Polka Dot and Yellow Daisy. The most sought-after pieces tend to be early hand-painted wares and lustrewares; services have also risen enormously in popularity in recent years.

◀ SHAPES
Wares are categorized according to their shape and the pattern with which they are decorated. This part-coffee set (c.1935) is in the Kestrel shape. Other popular forms include Curlew, Jay and Wren. $575–675 for the pieces shown

▶ DECORATION
Decoration on Susie Cooper is remarkably wide-ranging: floral designs, transfer prints, incised decoration and geometric patterns were all variously used. This pottery jug (c.1935) is carved with a charging goat, and covered in a moss green glaze. $180–270

MARKS
- Most Susie Cooper pieces are marked with a facsimile signature.
- Pieces can be dated both by mark and by serial number.
- Pieces made while Susie Cooper was working at A. E. Gray's may have both the company name and the designer's own initials.

POOLE POTTERY

Pottery has been made in the region of Poole in Dorset for centuries but the company now known as Poole Pottery was established by Jesse Carter in 1873. Among the earliest pieces it turned out were terracotta jardinières, some designed by Archibald Knox for retail through Liberty & Co, and lustrewares. Other designers who worked for Carter include James Radley Young who designed wares in an ethnic style, and Roger Fry whose designs were retailed through the Omega Workshops. In 1921 the company took on new partners Harold and Phoebe Stabler and John Adams to form a company known as Carter, Stabler & Adams. Other important designers at Poole are Truda Sharp (later Truda Carter), who produced colourful bold geometric and floral designs, and Olive Bourne, who produced plates decorated with stylized female faces. During the 1960s and 1970s the company continued to produce highly innovative studio wares.

◀ CARTER, STABLER & ADAMS
Under the influence of the new partners a range of sculptural pieces was introduced. Figures include "The Bull" and "Picardy Peasants". This roundel of the "Piping Faun" (1914) was designed by Phoebe Stabler. $2,250–3,000

MARKS
Poole pottery is invariably marked – a wide range of marks were used. They usually include the name of the company together with the decorator's initials or pattern code.

▶ ORNAMENTAL WARES
Among the most sought-after pieces of Poole pottery are the large hand-potted ornamental wares produced in the 1920s and 1930s. This large boldly painted jar and cover is signed by Truda Carter, one of Poole's leading designers. $4,500–6,000.

▶ ARCHITECTURAL CERAMICS
Architectural ceramics are among Poole's large and varied output. This tile advertising panel from the 1920s was made for the bookseller W. H. Smith, with lettering designed by the well-known illustrator Eric Gill. $750–900

DOULTON FIGURES

Doulton figures follow a long tradition of fig-urative ceramics and, although a few were made at the end of the 19th century by C. J. Noke, the vast majority were produced in the Burslem factory at some time between the 1920s and the present day. Extremely popular with collectors in both Britain and the United States, Doulton figures were produced in an enormously varied range of subjects. Figures are easily identifiable thanks to the marks and names on their bases. Each bears a series num-ber and the prefix "HN" and the factory records are also helpful as they can tell you for how long every design was produced. Pretty ladies in elegant dresses became one of the firm's specialities, as did bathing belles, figures in historic dress, animals, dancers, jesters and street vendors. Value depends on the rarity of the model and on the subject, and rare colour variations also command a premium.

▶ **THE PIED PIPER**
One of the more elaborately decorated Doulton figures is this "Modern Piper" (1925–38). Based on the Pied Piper of Hamelin, the piece is marked "HN 756". It commands a relatively high value which reflects the decorative appeal of the subject and the fact that the design was made for a relatively short time. $1,500–2,250

▼ **RARITY**
Lesley Harradine designed this rare and sought-after figure entitled "Scotties" and marked "HN 1281". It was introduced in 1928 and withdrawn in 1938. The Scottish terriers were a fashionable pet at the time; hence the subject's popularity. $2,250–3,000

◀ **SUBJECTS**
This naked figure entitled "The Bather" was produced in the 1920s and 1930s in several versions. In the 1930s a similar figure was also introduced, dressed in a swimming costume. The clothed figure is rare and therefore slightly more valuable than the naked one. Naked $900–1,200; clothed $1,200–1,800

CHARACTER JUGS

ANOTHER OF DOULTON'S MOST SUCCESSFUL 20TH-CENTURY PRODUCTS, CHARACTER JUGS CONTINUE THE TRADITION OF THE TOBY JUGS OF THE 18TH AND 19TH CENTURIES, AND WERE PRODUCED IN HUGE QUANTITIES FROM THE LATE 1930S ONWARDS. CHARACTER JUGS WERE OFTEN MADE IN FOUR DIFFERENT SIZES RANGING FROM LARGE, SMALL, MINIATURE AND TINY.

SUBJECTS INCLUDE FAMOUS PERSONALITIES OF THE PAST AND PRESENT. DICK TURPIN, OLD KING COLE, WINSTON CHURCHILL AND FRANCIS DRAKE HAVE BEEN REPRESENTED IN THIS WAY. VALUES ARE HIGHEST FOR RARE VARIATIONS WHICH CAN FETCH $4,500 OR MORE, ALTHOUGH THE MAJORITY FALL INTO THE $150–600 PRICE RANGE AND YOU CAN FIND RECENT EXAMPLES FOR UNDER $75.

MARKS

As with figures, jugs are marked and well documented. They are invariably named on the piece and bear the full factory mark, a date showing when the design was introduced and a "D" series number.

◀ **HANDLES**
The handles of Doulton character jugs are usually modelled to reflect the subject. This "Gondolier" (1964–69) has a handle appropriately modelled as a Venetian gondola. $300–450

▶ **VALUE**
Rarity rather than date has the biggest impact on value. This Alfred Hitchcock character jug is fairly recent in date (1995), but is a rare variation, because the shower curtain handle (a feature from the film *Psycho*) is pink; later versions, which are far more common, have a blue curtain. $900–1,200

WEDGWOOD

The tradition established by Josiah Wedgwood & Company of commissioning leading artists and illustrators to design ceramics for them was one established from the company's earliest days (see p70) and has continued unabated throughout the 20th century. As a result the company is responsible for some of the most distinctive of all British ceramic designs of the modern period. Designers include John Skeaping, Richard Guyatt, Keith Murray, Eric Ravilious, and Daisy Makeig-Jones. Twentieth-century Wedgwood has little uniformity of style and collectors tend to concentrate on the work of particular designers rather than the pottery as a whole. Value depends on the size and elaborateness of the decoration as well as on the reputation of the designer concerned.

◀ **DAISY MAKEIG- JONES**
One of the chief designers working for Wedgwood in the 1920s, Daisy Makeig-Jones designed the ornamental range known as "Fairyland lustre" – a variegated dark-coloured ground printed with colours and gilding depicting imaginary landscapes and fantastic figures. Although these pieces are in part mechanically produced, some of the rarer designs can attract very high prices. This vase is decorated with Woodland Bridge and Woodland Elves II patterns. Daisy Makeig-Jones also produced less elaborate, more modestly priced ranges of lustreware including "Dragon lustre" and "Butterfly lustre". $5,250–6,000

▶ **ERIC RAVILIOUS**
The illustrator Eric Ravilious produced a number of designs for Wedgwood in the 1930s including alphabet nursery ware, a zodiac set, a boat race cup and bowl, and a design for a commemorative tankard for the coronation of Edward VIII, which was adapted for the coronations of George VI and Elizabeth II. This nursery plate designed in 1937 is typical of his simple but effective designs. Ravilious himself was killed while working as a war artist in 1942, before many of the wares printed with his designs could be produced. $120–150

◄ KEITH MURRAY

Keith Murray was a prominent architect whom Wedgwood commissioned to create a range of more modern designs. Bold geometric shapes in muted shades and simple patterns are typical of his distinctive style. This bowl (c.1935) is a typically strong form with a plain off-white surface, made more stylish by the addition of a silver lustre glazed band inside the rim and on the foot. $375–450

MARKS

Works by designers are usually marked with a printed signature or the words "designed by..." plus the name and the Wedgwood mark. Letter date marks were also used; after 1929 the last two years of the date appear in full.

► OTHER DESIGNERS

A wide range of designers were employed by Wedgwood in the 20th century, and the value of their work depends on the appeal of the form. This jug (c.1910–30), designed by Alfred and Louise Powell, was made for commercial production and painted by hand. Rarely were ceramics of this type signed by the Powells. $150–180

▲ JOHN SKEAPING

Animals in matt glazes were the speciality of John Skeaping who produced designs in 1927 for Wedgwood for a group of ten different animals. Skeaping's subjects include deer, a polar bear, a kangaroo, a bison and monkeys in various glazes and he was paid $15 for each model. Animals are typically marked both with the designer's name and that of Wedgwood. Examples such as this sealion and calf fetch $450–600 each.

CARLTON

Carltonware was produced by the Carlton Works, based in Stoke-on-Trent. The company was founded in 1890 and renamed Carlton Ware Ltd in 1957. The pottery enjoyed a heyday of popularity during the 1920s and 1930s when it produced a huge range of decorative items and tablewares; geometric designs, moulded tablewares, novelty items and lustre decoration are particular specialities. The most desirable pieces tend to be those painted with bold abstract designs or lustre pieces decorated in Oriental style. Tablewares tend to be far less sought after than Carlton's decorative items. Prices range from $75–450 for small vessels to $1,500 and upwards for larger decorative pieces.

▶ **GUINESS ADVERTISING**
Objects advertising Guinness have a cult following among collectors. Although estimated at $300–600 for the set, these 1930s toucan wall plaques sold for over $1,500. Beware there are modern fakes of these.

▼ **DESIGNS**
Decorative items painted in distinctive abstract designs with bright colours are among the most highly sought after of all Carlton Ware items. This vase typifies the innovative patterns found on pieces of the 1930s; later colours tended to be more subdued. $450–600

▶ **ORIENTAL DESIGNS**
Lustrewares were produced in large quantities by the Carlton factory. Pieces such as this hexagonal covered vase made c.1930 reflect the influence of Oriental-style design both in their decoration and choice of shape. $300–450

MARKS
● Some early marks have the initials of Wiltshaw & Robinson as well as the name Carlton Ware.
● Designers are not generally named.

SHELLEY

First known as Wileman & Co, then as Foley, the Shelley factory is best known for the highly original Art Deco-style tablewares produced during the 1920s along with nursery wares and pieces based on Mabel Lucie Attwell figures. The most valuable pieces are Art Deco tablewares boldly painted with futuristic designs in very distinctive colour combinations. Less striking designs with floral decoration were produced during the 1930s and 1940s and these tend to be far less sought after. Shelley also produced commemorative pieces and their value depends mainly on the rarity of the design (see p140).

◄ VALUE
The streamlined geometric shape, futuristic design and bold yellow/black colour scheme combine to make this Sunray pattern part-coffee set (c.1930) extremely sought after. Wares are also categorized according to their shape. This form is known as Mode; other shapes are Eve, Vogue, Queen Anne and Regent. $450–750 (for the pieces shown)

► FIGURES
Shelley also produced a popular range of figurines and nursery wares, which are keenly sought after, based on the illustrations of Mabel Lucie Attwell. This group (c.1937) is known as "Our Pets" and features children with their pet rabbits. It is rare and therefore more valuable than more common subjects. $1,200–1,800

MARKS
Pieces are usually marked with a signature in a cartouche and serial number. Marks which include the words "Fine Bone China", date from after 1945. A serial number beginning with a 2 shows the piece was a second.

► LATER DESIGNS
The more elaborate designs of the 1930s and later tend to fetch considerably less than those in the Art Deco style and are still available for modest sums. This part-tea service (c.1928), attractively decorated with a landscape design, contains more than 20 individual pieces and would be worth $330–420.

WADE FIGURES

Famous for its range of endearing porcelain and cellulose nursery figures and animals, the Wade factory was founded in 1922 in Burslem, Staffordshire, by George Wade. The company also established a factory in Ireland where it made porcelain for the tourist industry and export market. Price generally depends on the rarity and popularity of the subject. The most sought-after early Disney figures of the 1930s can fetch $2,250. Pieces modelled by Faust Lang, a leading Wade modeller, are also keenly sought after and command a premium, but you will still find animals and other figures for under $1.

MARKS

Figures are not always marked and do not have serial numbers. To help identify and date figures, refer to the specialist collectors' guides on the subject listed on pp168–9.

◀ DISNEY FIGURES

Disney figures were produced to coincide with new films and are still being produced today. This figure depicts Tramp from the film *Lady and the Tramp* and was produced between 1961 and 1965. $112–150

▼ OTHER SUBJECTS

Apart from animal figures Wade produced a wide range of other small decorative objects including models of Pearly Kings and Queens, the latter (c.1959) shown here, advertising wares, novelty egg cups, vases, money boxes, jugs and trays. Most of these are less valuable than the figures. $60–90

▲ ANIMALS

A vast range of endearing animals such as this seal were produced by Wade in the 1950s. Condition does affect value, however, so look out for small chips and imperfections which will reduce the price quite significantly. $70–150

CELLULOSE FIGURES

A range of inexpensive cellulose figures were produced by Wade in the 1930s. These are especially vulnerable to flaking paint and prices are lower than for ceramic figures from other factories.

BESWICK FIGURES

The pottery-making company founded in the late 19th century by James Beswick was taken over by his son in 1920 and sold to Royal Doulton in 1969. Since the 1920s it has established a reputation for its popular range of decorative china animals. Subjects include figurines depicting animals from Beatrix Potter and Winnie the Pooh. The firm has also produced a range of figures of animals and birds as well as low-relief wall plaques in graduated sets. Horses are a particular favourite with collectors and some figures portray named jockeys with well-known racehorses. The highest prices tend to be paid for rare popular subjects – a series of Beatrix Potter wall plaques made in 1967–69 can fetch over $1,800 each, and even figures produced in the 1980s can make over $150.

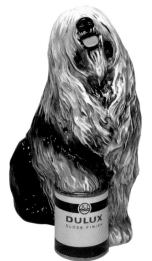

◀ DATING
Pieces can be dated from the mark and model by referring to the specialist guides on the subject listed on pp168–9. This Old English sheepdog, "The Dulux dog", was produced between 1964 and 1970. $180–225

▲ HORSES
Model horses are extremely popular with collectors and from the 1950s onwards the firm employed some highly skilled modellers to produce their designs. The Canadian Mountie on a prancing horse shown here is typically finely worked. The group was modelled by Arthur Gredington and produced between 1955 and 1976. $225–240.

▼ VALUE
Among the most sought-after Beswick figures are Beatrix Potter subjects, Alice in Wonderland figures and this set representing Snow White and the Seven Dwarfs, produced 1954–67. $1,500–2,250

STUDIO CERAMICS

One of the most dramatic recent develop-ments in the world of ceramics is the rise of interest in post-war studio pottery. Individually hand-crafted pieces by certain leading potters have enjoyed a rapid increase in popularity and price in recent decades, but value depends on quality rather than upon the name of the potter concerned and only a handful command high prices.

Bernard Leach is regarded by many as the founder of the revival in British studio ceram-ics. After a visit to Japan where he met the potter Shoji Hamada and became fascinated by Oriental ceramics, Leach with Hamada established a factory at St Ives in 1920 which influenced and inspired a generation of stu-dent potters. Lucie Rie is perhaps the best known of all the studio potters; she trained in Vienna in her native Austria and came to London in 1938 where she initially earned her living making buttons. Rie along with Hans Coper with whom she worked closely from 1946, are renowned for their strong innovative forms and unusual glazes.

◀ BERNARD LEACH
Made during the early years of Leach's St Ives pottery, this slipware dish reflects the influence of traditional slipware techniques in the vein of Thomas Toft (see p62) and was made by dipping the earthenware body in a creamy slip and trailing designs in darker slip on top. $4,500–7,500

▶ DESIGN
The influence of Oriental design can be seen on this Bernard Leach stoneware flask which is decorated with calligraphic motifs against a soft grey and blue quartered background. Leach's work is always thickly potted and simple in form. $1,500–2,250

◀ HANS COPER
Unusual shapes with little additional decoration are a hall-mark of many of Hans Coper's vases. This stoneware "Thistle" vase made c.1950 is characteristically finished with a pale finely textured surface and a contrasting brownish black interior. $12,000–15,000

◄ **VALUE**
Size, rarity and decorative appeal all play a part in determining value. This fine green porcelain bowl (c.1983) with a bronze glazed band by Lucie Rie is a highly decorative object, and even though it is only 6 ¾in (17cm) in diameter it sold for $9,488.

MARKS
- **Bernard Leach** usually marked with "BL" either painted, impressed monogram or cipher.
- **Lucie Rie** an impressed seal of "LR" monogram.
- **Hans Coper** an impressed "HC" cipher resembling a potter's wheel on its side.

► **LUCIE RIE**
This tapering stoneware vase (c.1974) by Lucie Rie is decorated with mottled glazes, reflecting her fascination with different glaze techniques, which she often used to give texture to the surface of her pots. $1,200–1,800

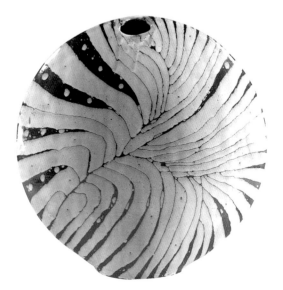

◄ **OTHER POTTERS**
This circular earthenware vessel (1983) is by James Tower, one of a new generation of studio potters whose work is increasingly collectable. Other potters whose work is also achieving notable success include Elizabeth Fritsch, Sue Mundy, Alison Britton, Gabriele Koch and Abdo Nagi. $3,750–5,250

The development of the American ceramic industry was hampered by the fashion for imported foreign wares and a shortage of skilled manpower. Foreign wares had always been considered superior and provided the inspiration for most early American ceramics. The first American porcelains are hard to distinguish from the imported wares they copied and are rarely marked. Wares made by Bonnin & Morris in Philadelphia from 1770–72 copied Bow; Tucker porcelains made in Philadelphia from 1826–38 were based on French 18th-century designs; D. & H. Henderson's Jersey City stonewares are mistaken for those made by Ridgway; brown-glazed wares from Bennington, Vermont, are similar to Derby wares; while Belleek made in Trenton rivalled Irish Belleek and Royal Worcester.

Despite the gradual burgeoning of potteries in the 19th century, American ceramics shown at the great Centennial Exposition in Philadelphia in 1876 received little notice. Since the turn of the century, however, interest in American ceramics has grown, and collectors now prefer these rarer American versions, and pay a premium for them. Among the most popular are 18th-century slip-decorated redwares, produced from c.1750 onwards in New England, and salt-glazed stonewares developed by immigrant French and German potters from c.1750. English imported pottery such as spatterware is also becoming increasingly popular. Innovative forms and decorations are hallmarks of art pottery made from the late 19th century and this is avidly collected too.

EARLY AMERICAN CERAMICS

America's first porcelain factory, Bonnin & Morris, was founded by the British-born Gousse Bonnin and the Philadelphian Antony Morris in Philadelphia in 1769. The factory produced dinner- and teawares in underglaze blue and polychrome decoration for only two years. After that the Non-Importation Act restricting British imports was repealed. Wares are extremely rare and expensive. The second American porcelain manufacturer, William Ellis Tucker, was in business from 1826–38. Much is unmarked and hard to distinguish from the French and Italian prototypes on which it is based. The mid-19th century English fashion for Parian figures quickly crossed the Atlantic and Parian was produced in Bennington, Vermont, the Greenpoint section of Brooklyn, and Trenton, New Jersey.

▲ **BONNIN & MORRIS**
This pickle stand (1770–72) was the company's most expensive form. Based on similar pieces made at Plymouth and Bow, London it reflects the great rarity of all Bonnin & Morris porcelain. Only two pickle stands have been sold in recent decades; one bought at a tag sale for $2 sold for over $66,000; this one sold for $82,500 in 1989.

► **TUCKER PORCELAIN**

Tucker produced a wide range of tablewares and decorative objects. The undecorated coffee pot is a rare form. The three-vase garniture is decorated with floral decoration on one side and sepia scenes on the other (1828–38). Coffee pot $5,000–8,000; pitchers $1,500–5,000 each; garniture $20,000–25,000

▼ **VALUE**

The vase-shaped pitcher is a form unique to Tucker and was produced with a variety of decoration; prices depend on the painting – Philadelphia views are particularly sought after. This example (c.1830), painted on either side with sprays of flowers, is identified as No. 7 in the Tucker pattern book and it sold for $6,325.

► **PARIAN**

This marked bust of William Shakespeare (c.1876) was produced by Ott & Brewer, Parian manufacturers of Trenton, New Jersey, who produced a range of busts including George Washington, Abraham Lincoln, Ulysses Grant, Benjamin Franklin and Cleopatra, all by the sculptor Isaac Broome. $7,000–10,000 (less if small or unmarked)

IDENTIFICATION & MARKS

• Bonnin & Morris pieces are unmarked or simply marked with a letter "P".

• Most Tucker is unmarked; some pieces are marked "Tucker and Hulme" or "Tucker and Hemphill". Early examples can be identified by their greenish cast when held up to the light. Later pieces seem orange or straw-coloured.

AMERICAN ART POTTERY I

The nationwide fashion for painted ceramics in the years following the Centennial Exhibition gave rise to the American Art Pottery movement, which flourished from c.1875–1920. Two prominent Cincinnati women were largely responsible for its development. Mary Louise McLoughlin created Cincinnati faience, based on the slip-painted wares of Limoges and on Japanese wares, and founded the Cincinnati Pottery Club. Maria Longworth Nichols established the Rookwood Pottery in 1880 and by 1890 was offering "standard" wares slip-cast and decorated in dark brown, red, orange and yellow under a yellow-tinted high-gloss glaze; Iris and Sea Green glazes in 1894; and matte glazes by 1902. The most desirable pieces are those signed by artists; over 100 decorators marked with their initials or a cipher. Other prominent American Art potteries include Grueby of Boston, the Dedham pottery, Massachusetts, and the Newcomb pottery, founded in 1895 at Sophie Newcomb Memorial College for Women in New Orleans by Mary G. Sheerer.

► **GRUEBY**

William Grueby of Boston specialized in organic forms decorated with matte glazes in green, yellow, ochre and brown. His most popular works have crisp applied decorations in the form of leaves and buds. The Grueby pottery was patronized by Gustav Stickley, a leader of the Arts and Crafts movement. These vases were made c.1900. From left to right: $8,000; $5,000; $7,500

ROOKWOOD MARKS

Rookwood is impressed with the "RP" mark. A flame over the mark was introduced in 1886, and another flame added each year until 1900 when a Roman numeral was added to indicate the year. Many pieces are also signed by their artists, and these are much sought after.

◄ **ROOKWOOD**

The influence of Japanese design on Rookwood pottery became more prevalent after the arrival of the young Japanese artist Kataro Shirayamadani in 1887. This ovoid vellum landscape vase (c.1920) was decorated by Edward Diers, another prominent Rookwood artist. Vellum, a matte glaze transparent enough to be used over coloured slip decorations, was introduced in 1904. $1,800–$2,500

◀ NEWCOMB

These Newcomb vases (c.1900-1908) are typically decorated with designs based on the flora and fauna of the surrounding bayou country. The decoration is created by drawing into the wet clay and painting with oxides after the first firing. Wares were then given a transparent high-gloss glaze in a distinctive palette of blue, green, yellow and black. Designs were rarely repeated. From left to right $15,000; $38,000; $18,000; $20,000 (damaged $5,000)

▶ DEDHAM

Oriental ceramics and French art pottery provided the inspiration for the Dedham pottery. Hugh Robertson, the pottery's founder, developed a wide variety of decorative effects including flambé and volcanic glazes and a dragon's blood finish, as well as crackle glazes decorated with blue and white borders of various animals marching clockwise. This crackle-glazed teapot (1896–1928) has a charming rabbit pattern and is marked with a blue stamp reading "Dedham Pottery" above a rabbit enclosed in a square frame. $800–1,200

◀ VAN BRIGGLE

Artus van Briggle, a decorator at Rookwood, set up his own pottery in Colorado Springs in 1901. Influenced by Art Nouveau his designs combine figural, floral and plant forms. This Lorelei vase reflects the influence of Rodin and was produced at Rookwood by van Briggle in 1898. $18,000–25,000

BEWARE

The van Briggle pottery still produces Lorelei vases. New ones sell for around $100; those from the late 1920s, called "dirty bottom ware" fetch around $1,000. Always buy from a reputable source or check against a known original if you are at all in doubt.

AMERICAN ART POTTERY II

Other leading American art potters include Louis Comfort Tiffany, Teco, Fulper and George Ohr. Pottery became an interest for Tiffany in 1904, long after his reputation as an interior designer was established. Pieces were typically cast in Art Nouveau style but Tiffany's pottery proved to be less successful than his glass and was discontinued after 1917. One of the United States' most prolific potters was George Ohr, "the Mad Potter from Biloxi", who made more than 10,000 pots of unparalleled virtuosity and crammed them into barrels in the family attic. Regarded today as the father of the studio pottery movement, Ohr produced innovative forms that anticipate many of the developments of contemporary ceramics. The American Terracotta and Ceramic Company, known as Teco or as the Gates Pottery, registered a trademark in 1895 and is especially known for its architectual ceramics, some designed by Frank Lloyd Wright. The Fulper Pottery Co in Flemington, New Jersey, was established in 1815 and produced stoneware and utilitarian earthenware before turning to art pottery. William Hill Fulper made moulded or hand-thrown stoneware in Classical and Oriental forms and used a variety of glazes.

◀ ▲ TIFFANY

Tiffany pottery was mostly made by casting into moulds. Organic forms and decoration reflect the Art Nouveau style. Light yellow-green tones were favoured on early pieces. The baluster vase left (c.1912) has a textured semi-gloss glaze, while the vase above (c.1910) with embossed foliage is matte-glazed. Left $1,200–1,500; above $2,000–2,500

▶ TECO

The silvery matte green glaze seen on this floor vase (c.1905) is typical of Teco pottery and was inspired by matte glazes on French ceramics shown at the 1893 World's Columbian Exposition in Chicago. Teco mass-produced 500 shapes in various matte colours including brown, grey, blue, rose, purple and yellow. The innovative architectural form is characteristic of this company's ceramics. Teco is marked with a long-stemmed "T" with the "e", "c' and "o" arranged under each other. $10,000–15,000

▶ FULPER

Fulper pottery lamps were patented in 1912. This example (c.1915) has a ceramic base and shade with yellow and green slag glass inserts mounted with copper foil. The lamp is decorated with a crystalline dark leopard skin glaze in brown, cream and grey.
$10,000–15,000

MARKS

Fulper is usually marked with an impressed name but is rarely dated. Vertical letters are earlier than horizontal ones. A circular mark with the date of 1805 is sometimes seen.

▼ GEORGE OHR

Unctuous glazes richly mottled in metallic colours, bizarre forms and thin walls are distinctive features of George Ohr's pottery. Pieces such as these vases (c.1905–1910) are impressed "GEO E OHR/BILOXI, MISS." Left to right $1,500–$2,500; $7,500–10,000; $4,500–5,500

EARTHENWARE & STONEWARE

Red earthenware pottery was made by the earliest settlers at Jamestown, Virginia, and Plymouth, Massachusetts. In the South, as the plantation owners prospered, slave-made pottery was relegated to the kitchen while imported wares were used on the table by the masters. In New England and the Middle States there was also demand for storage and kitchen wares made by local potters. Before the end of the 17th century potters decorated their wares with simple slip-trailed designs. Inspired by the folk pottery of the Rhine Valley and Switzerland, sgraffito and slip-

decorated redware reached its fullest flowering on ornamental pie plates. Stoneware was also produced in the United States by such potters as Remmey and Crolius in New York and Norton in Bennington, Vermont. Among a wide range of stoneware objects made were crocks, jugs, jars, chamber pots, colanders, butter tubs and pitchers, often decorated with incised or painted cobalt blue designs. Various new types of stoneware were developed in the 19th century including brown-glazed Rockingham ware and flint enamel, a process developed by C. W. Fenton in Bennington.

▶ **REDWARE**
This redware jar made in Pennsylvania in the late 18th century is typically decorated with a slip design of tulips. This form of decoration is identified with Conrad Mumbouer of Haycock Township, Bucks County (1794–1844). Decorated hollow wares such as this command a premium with collectors; hence the high valu $17,000–18,500

▼ **STONEWARE**
This 19th-century salt-glazed stoneware pitcher is decorated in cobalt blue and is stamped by John Bell of the Bell Pottery, Waynesboro, Shenandoah Valley, Pennsylvania (1833–89). Decoration determines value; jugs and crocks with cobalt floral decoration are less valuable than those with figures, birds and animals. Incised designs bring a premium. $1,500–2,500

◀ **SGRAFFITO**
This redware plate (c.1805) has been covered with white slip and the design created by scratching through to the red clay, a technique known as sgraffito. The figure on horseback is surrounded by an inscription in a German dialect which translates as: "I have ridden over hill and dale and found girls everywhere". Plates decorated with figures are rare and expensive; this plate is worth over $75,000. Floral decorated plates are more readily available and cost from $1,500.

ANGLO-AMERICAN WARES

Quantities of hand-painted and transfer-printed ceramics were made in England in the 19th century for export to the United States. Not long after transfer printing was discovered, potteries in Liverpool made jugs, mugs, bowls and plates decorated with sailing ships and patriotic subjects that would appeal to visiting seamen. Staffordshire potters also produced pitchers with transfer-printed naval battles and portraits of heroes. After the war of 1812, hundreds of different American views were transfer-printed in underglaze blue on various domestic items (see p78). English potters also produced hand-decorated pearlware for export, imitating Imari patterns made at Derby and Worcester. Popular with Pennsylvanian Germans, these colourful wares are known as "Gaudy Dutch".

◀ LIVERPOOL POTTERY
Made at the Herculaneum pottery in Liverpool c.1769–1800, this jug is decorated with a transfer print of *Peace, Plenty and Independence*. On the reverse side there is a print of a ship flying an American flag. Jugs with patriotic designs range from $1,500–20,000. This one is particularly valuable because it is hand-coloured and in mint condition; it sold for $18,000.

▲ "GAUDY DUTCH"
"Gaudy Dutch" came in several patterns including Butterfly, Grape, War Bonnet, Single Rose, Oyster, Zinnia, Carnation and Sunflower. This cup (1830–50) is an example of the Butterfly pattern. All "Gaudy Dutch" designs are hand-painted in a distinctive palette of orange, yellow, green and red with underglaze blue. $900–1,200

▶ BLUE & WHITE TRANSFER-PRINTED WARES
Blue and white wares decorated with American subjects were produced in Staffordshire for export. This soup tureen (c.1830) featuring Pennsylvania Hospital would be worth about $8,500. Plates start at around $200.

◀ SPATTERWARE
Produced by Staffordshire potters from 1820–1860, spatterware was another popular type of export pottery. It came in a wide range of colours often with an image and a spatter border. Pieces such as these are rare and costly. The rainbow spatter teapot and bowl sold for $16,000; the pitcher for $11,500.

PART 5

INFORMATION

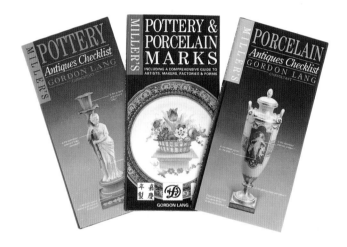

ABOVE A VALUABLE SOURCE ON PRICES.

LEFT VIEWING AND EXAMINING THE CERAMICS ON
OFFER PRIOR TO A SALE.

WHERE TO BUY

Contact the following trade associations for information on antique shows and specialist dealers:

National Art & Antiques Dealers' Association (NAADA)
12 East 56th Street
New York NY 10022

Art and Antique Dealers' League
353 East 78th Street
New York NY 10022

International Foundation for Art Research (IFAR)
500 5th Avenue
Suite 1234
New York
NY 10110

British Antique Dealers' Association (BADA)
20 Rutland Gate
London SW7 1BD
England

AMERICAN AUCTION HOUSES

Ronald Bourgeault
Northeast Auctions
P.O. Box 363
Hampton
NH 03842

Butterfield & Butterfield
220 San Bruno Avenue
San Francisco
CA 94103

Christie's
502 Park Avenue
New York NY 10022

Christie's East
219 E 67th Street
New York NY 10021

William Doyle Galleries
175 E 87th Street
New York NY 19028

Ken Farmer Auctions and Estates
105 A Harrison Street
Radford VA 24141

Garth's Auctions
2690 Stratford Road
Box 369
Delaware
OH 43015

Leslie Hindman Auctioneers
215 West Ohio Street
Chicago IL 60610

Pook & Pook
P.O. Box 268
Downington
PA 19335

David Rago Auctions Inc.
333 North Main Street
Lambertville
New Jersey 08530

Skinner Inc.
Route 117
Bolton MA

C G Sloan & Co.
4950 Wyaconda Road
North Betheda
MD 20852

Sotheby's
1334 York Avenue
New York NY 10021

Treadway Gallery
2029 Madison Road
Cincinnati OH 45208

MAJOR ANTIQUES SHOWS

JANUARY
New York Winter Antiques Show
Seventh Regiment
Armory
67th Street and
Park Avenue
New York NY 10021

Dorchester Antiques Fair
Dorchester Hotel
Park Lane
London W1
England

FEBRUARY
Stella's Manhattan Triple Pier Exposition
Passenger Piers
'88 '90 '92
New York 10019
(also in November)

MARCH
Wendy's Armory Antiques Show
(March, May
September and
December)
Seventh Regiment
Armory
67th Street and
Park Avenue
New York NY 10021

Wilton Historical Society Show
Wilton High School
Field House
Wilton
CT 06897

Chester County Historical Society Show
Hollinger Field House
West Chester University
West Chester
PA 19380

International Asian Art Fair
Seventh Regiment
Armory
67th Street and
Park Avenue
New York NY 10021

APRIL
Philadelphia Antiques Show
103rd Engineers
Armory
33rd and
Market Streets
Philadelphia PA 19104

British International Antiques Fair
National Exhibition
Centre
Birmingham
West Midlands
England

MAY
Jim Burk's Greater York Antiques Show
York Fairgrounds
West Market Street
York PA 17401

JUNE

The Grosvenor House Art & Antiques Fair
Grosvenor House Hotel
Park Lane
London W1
England

Fine Art & Antiques Fair
Olympia
Kensington
London W14
England

AUGUST

New Hampshire Antique Dealers Association Show
Center of New Hampshire
Holiday Inn
Manchester
NH 03101

Riverside Antiques Show
New Hampshire State Armory
Canal Street
Manchester NH 03101

Mid-Week Manchester Antiques Show
Sheraton Tara
Wayfarer Inn
Bedford NH

Vermont Antique Dealers Show
Stratton Mountain
Base Lodge
Bondville
VT 05340

National Exhibition Centre
(August Fair)
Birmingham
West Midlands
England

West London Antiques Fair
Kensington Town Hall
Hornton Street
London W8
England

SEPTEMBER

Fall Show at the Armory
67th Street and Park Avenue
New York
NY 10021

City Antique & Fine-Art Fair
The Business Design Centre
Islington
London N1
England

OCTOBER

Antiquarian and Landmark Society Antiques
State Armory
Hartford
CT 96105

International Fine Art and Antique Dealers Show
Seventh Regiment Armory
67th Street and Park Avenue
New York
NY 10021

San Francisco Fall Antiques Show
Fort Mason Center
Festival Pavilion
San Francisco
CA 94123

LAPADA Antiques Fair
The Royal College of Art
Kensington Gore
London SW7
England

NOVEMBER

Delaware Antiques Show
Tatnall School
1501 Barley Mill Road
Wilmington DE 19807

Modernism
Seventh Regiment Armory
67th Street and Park Avenue
New York
NY 10021

SPECIALIST DEALERS

Cincinnati Art Galleries
635 Main Street
Cincinnati
Ohio 45202

Bea Cohen
Box 825
Easton
PA 18044 0825

Sidney Gecker
225 West 21st Street
New York NY 10011

James and Nancy Glazer
1308 Mt. Pleasant Road
Villanova
PA 19085

Harry B. Hartman
452 East Front Street
Marietta
PA 17547

Hirschl and Adler
21 East 70th Street
New York
NY 10021

William Kurau Jr.
P O Box
457 Lampeter
PA 17537

Chris and Corine Machmer
146 West Main Street
Annville
PA 17003

The Stradlings
1225 Park Ave
New York
NY 10128

Walters-Benisek
One Amber Lane
Northampton
MA 01060

WHERE TO SEE

There are many places where you can study and see antiques – such as museums, historical societies and house museums. Some of the most interesting are listed below:

CALIFORNIA
Los Angeles
County Museum
of Art
59905 Wilshire Blvd
Los Angeles CA 90036

California Palace of
the Legion of Honor
Lincoln Park
34th and Clement
San Francisco
CA 94121

CONNECTICUT
Wadsworth
Athenaeum
600 Main Street
Hartford CT 06103

DELAWARE
Winterthur Museum
and Gardens
Winterthur DE 19735

DISTRICT OF
COLUMBIA
National Museum
of American History
Smithsonian
Institute
Constitution Avenue
12th–14th Streets
Washington DC
20560

GEORGIA
High Museum
of Art
1280 Peachtree
Street NE
Atlanta GA 39349

ILLINOIS
Art Institute of
Chicago
Michigan Avenue at
Adams Street
Chicago IL 60603

MARYLAND
Baltimore Museum
of Art
Art Museum Drive
Baltimore MD 21218

Maryland Historical
Society
201 West Monument
Street Baltimore
MD 21218

MASSACHUSETTS
Concord Museum
200 Lexington Road
P. O. Box 146
Concord MA 01742

Historic Deerfield
Box 321
Deerfield
MA 01342

Museum of Fine
Arts Boston
46 Huntingdon
Avenue
Boston MA 02115

Old Sturbridge
Village
1 Old Sturbridge
Village Road
Sturbridge
MA 015662

Peabody Essex
Museum
Liberty and
Essex Streets
Salem
MA 01970

MICHIGAN
The Detroit
Institute
of Arts
5200 Woodward
Avenue
Detroit
MI 48202

The Henry Ford
Museum and
Greenfield Village
20900 Oakwood Blvd
Dearborn MI 48121

MINNESOTA
Minneapolis
Institute of Arts
2400 Third Avenue
South Minneapolis
MN 55404

MISSOURI
Nelson-Atkins
Musum of Art
4525 Oak Street
Kansas City
MO 64111

St. Louis Art
Museum
1 Fine Arts Drive
St. Louis
MO 63110

NEW HAMPSHIRE
Currier Gallery
of Art
19 Orange Street
Manchester
NH 03801

Strawbery Banke
Marcy Street
P. O. Box 300
Portsmouth NH 03801

NEW JERSEY
Newark Museum
49 Washington Street
Newark NJ 07101

NEW YORK
Brooklyn Museum
200 Eastern Parkway
Brooklyn
New York NY 11236

Cooper Hewitt
National Museum
of Design
Smithsonian Institute
3 East 91st Street
New York NY 10128

Everson Museum
of Art
401 Harrison Street
Syracuse
New York NY 13202

Metropolitan
Museum of Art
Fifth Avenue at
82nd Street
New York NY 10028

Museum of the
City of New York
1220 Fifth Avenue at
103rd Street
New York NY 10029

NORTH CAROLINA
Museum of
Early Southern
Decorative Arts
924 South Main Street
Old Salem
NC 27101

OHIO
Cleveland Museum
of Art
11150 East Blvd
Cleveland
OH 44106

PENNSYLVANIA
Philadelphia
Museum of Art
26th and Benjamin
Franklin Parkway
Philadelphia
PA 19103
(including the
Colonial Houses at
Fairmount Park)

Carnegie Museum
of Art
4400 Forbes Avenue
Pittsburgh
PA 15213

RHODE ISLAND
Museum of Art
Rhode Island
School of Design
224 Benefit Street
Providence
RI 02903

The Preservation
Society of
Newport County
P. O. Box 510
Newport
RI 02804

SOUTH
CAROLINA
Charleston
Museum
764 Meeting Street
Charleston
SC
(and three historic
houses)

TEXAS
Dallas Museum
of Art
1717 N. Harwood
Dallas TX 75291

Bayou Bend
Museum and
Gardens
1 Westcott
Houston TX 77007

VERMONT
Shelburne Museum
Route 7 Burlington
VT 05482

Bennington Museum
West Main Street
Bennington
VT 05201

VIRGINIA
The Chrysler
Museum
24 W Olney Road
Norfolk
VA 23510-1567

Virgina Museum
of Fine Arts
2800 Grove Avenue
Richmond
VA 23221-2466

Colonial
Williamsburg
P. O. Box C
Williamsburg
VA 23187

WISCONSIN
Milwaukee Art
Museum
759 North Lincoln
Memorial Drive
Milwaukee WI 53202

CANADA
Musée des Beaux
Arts de Montreal
1380 Sherbrook Street
Montreal
Canada

National Gallery
of Canada
380 Sussex Drive
Ottawa
Ontario
Canada

GREAT BRITAIN
Burghley House
Stamford
Lincolnshire
England

Chatsworth
Bakewell
Derbyshire
England

Geffrye Museum
Kingsland Road
Hackney
London
England

Houghton Hall
Houghton
Norfolk
England

Longleat House
Warminster
Wiltshire
England

Osterley Park
Osterley
Iselworth
Middlesex
England

Victoria &
Albert Museum
Cromwell Road
London SW7
England

WHAT TO READ

GENERAL

Atterbury, Paul, *History of Porcelain*, 1982

Battie, David, Ed., *Sotheby's Concise Encyclopedia of Porcelain*, 1990

Berges, Ruth, *From Gold to Porcelain; the Art of Porcelain and Faience*, 1963

Cushion, John, *Porcelain*, 1973

Charleston, Robert, Ed., *World Ceramics*, 1981

Fleming, John and Honour, Hugh, *The Penguin Dictionary of the Decorative Arts*, 1977

Honey, W. B., *The Art of the Potter*, 1980 and *Ceramic Art from the End of the Middle Ages to about 1815,* 1952

Knowles, Eric, *Miller's Antiques Checklists: Victorianna (*1991*), Art Nouveau (*1992*), Art Deco* (1991)

Lang, Gordon, *Miller's Antiques Checklists: Porcelain (*1991*), Pottery (*1995*), Pottery & Porcelain Marks (*1995*)*

Morley Fletcher, Hugo, Ed., *Techniques of the World's Great Masters of Pottery and Ceramics,* 1984

Savage, George, *Porcelain through the Ages*, 1954

Savage, George & Newman, Harold, *An Illustrated Dictionary of Ceramics*, 1958

EUROPEAN, ISLAMIC & AMERICAN CERAMICS

Atterbury, Paul, *Moorcroft Pottery*, 1987 and *Dictionary of Minton*, 1989

Austwick, J. and B., *The Decorated Tile*, 1980

Barber, Edwin Atlee, *The Pottery and Porcelain of the United States* 1909 (3rd edition); *Marks of American Potters*, 1904 and *Tulip ware of the Pennsylvania German Potters,* 1903

Barnard, J., *Victorian Ceramic Tiles*, 1972

Batkin, Maureen, *Wedgwood Ceramics 1846–1959*, 1982

Bergesen, V., *Majolica – British, Continental and American Wares*, 1989

Birks, Tony, *Lucie Rie*, 1987

Caiger-Smith, A., *Tin Glaze Pottery in Europe and the Islamic World*, 1973

Bivins Jr., John, *The Moravian Potters in North Carolina*, 1972

Clark, Garth and Hughto, Margie, *A Century of Ceramics in the United States 1878–1978*, 1979

Clark, Garth, Ellison Jr., Robert A. and Hecht, Eugene, *The Mad Potter of Biloxi; the Art & Life of George E. Ohr*, 1989

Comstock, H.E., *The Pottery of the Shenandoah Valley Region*, 1994

Cox and Cox, *Rockingham Pottery and Porcelain*, 1983

Cushion, J. B. *British Ceramic Marks*, 1988

Danckert, Ludwig, *Directory of European Porcelain*, 1981

Dennis, Richard, *Doulton Stoneware and Terracotta 1870–1925; Doulton Pottery Lambeth to Burslem 1873–1939*, 1975; *Royal Doulton 1815–1965*, 1965 and *The Parian Phenomenon*, 1989

Eidelberg, Martin, Editor, *From Our Native Clay, Art pottery from the Collections of the American Ceramics Arts Society,* 1987

Evans, Paul, *Art Pottery of the United States,* 1987
Eyles and Dennis, *Royal Doulton Figures,* 1978

Frelinghuysen, Alice Cooney, *American Porcelain 1770–1920,* 1989

Gilbert, Alfred, *English Art Pottery 1865–1915,* 1975

Godden, G. A., *Encyclopedia of British Pottery and Porcelain Marks,* 1994;
An Illustrated Encyclopedia of British Pottery and Porcelain, 1968;
The Illustrated Guide to Mason's Ironstone China, 1971;
Staffordshire Porcelain, 1983 and
Victorian Porcelain, 1961

Haggar, R. G., *Staffordshire Chimney Ornaments,* 1955

Hall, J., *Staffordshire Portrait Figures,* 1972

Haslam, Malcolm, *English Art Pottery 1865–1915,* 1975

Henzke, L. *American Art Pottery,* 1970

Hughes, Bernard G., *English and Scottish Earthenware; Victorian Pottery and Porcelain,* 1959

Lane, A., *Early Islamic Pottery*1947;
Later Islamic Pottery, 1957

Lloyd, Thomas E., *Victorian Art Pottery,* 1974

Oliver, A., *The Victorian Staffordshire Figure,* 1971

Rago, David, *The Fulper Book,* 1986

Rice, Paul and Gowing, Christopher, *British Studio Ceramics in the 20th Century,* 1989

Sandon, H., *The Illustrated Guide to Worcester Porcelain,* 1970

Sandon, H. and Grainger, J., *Worcester Porcelain,* 1989
Snyder, Jeffrey B., *Historical Staffordshire, American Patriots and Views,* 1995

Watson, Howard, *Collecting Clarice Cliff,* 1988

Wills, Geoffrey, *Wedgwood,* 1989

Wilson, T., *Ceramic Art of the Italian Renaissance,* 1987

Winstone, Victor, *Royal Copenhagen,* 1984

ORIENTAL

Beurdeley, M., and Raindre, G., *Qing Porcelain; Famille Verte, Famille Rose,* 1987

Carswell, John, *Chinese Blue and White and its Impact on the Western World,* 1985

Garner, Henry, *Oriental Blue and White,* 1970

Godden, G. A., *Oriental Export Market Porcelains,* 1979

Jenyns, Soame, *Japanese Pottery,* 1971 and *Japanese Porcelain,* 1985

Medley, Margaret, *The Art of the Chinese Potter,* 1981

Munsterberg, Hugo, *The Ceramic Art of Japan,* 1964

Reichel, Friedrich, *Early Japanese Porcelain,* 1981

Sato, M., *Chinese Ceramics, A Short History,* 1981

Vainker, S. J., *Chinese Pottery & Porcelain,* 1991

GLOSSARY

Agateware Pottery resembling the marbled effect of agate made in Staffordshire in the 18th century by mixing together clays of various colours.

Albarello Drug jar usually of waisted cylindrical form.

Applied decoration Ornamental motifs made separately from the main body and attached to it to provide decoration.

Arita Region in the West of Japan where the early porcelain industry was centred: Imari, blue«e and white, Kakiemon and Nabeshima were all produced in the area.

Armorial wares Pieces embellished with heraldic coats of arms, or crests.

Baluster Bulbous vase-shaped form.

Basalt ware (or Basaltes) Type of black stoneware developed by Josiah Wedgwood in the 1760s.

Basket weave Low relief motif simulating woven twigs or reeds.

Bat printing Printing decoration made using glutinous bats (sheets) popular in the early 19th century in Staffordshire.

Bellarmine Bulbous, narrow-necked German stoneware jug with a moulded mark, named after Cardinal Roberto Bellarmino.

Birnkrug Pear-shaped vessels originally from the Netherlands or Germany.

Biscuit Pottery or porcelain fired once but unglazed.

Blackware Iron rich type of ancient Chinese pottery.

Blanc de Chine Uncoloured, thickly glazed Chinese porcelain produced from the Ming dynasty.

Bleu celeste A sky blue enamel ground colour developed in the Vincennes factory in 1752 and particularly associated with Sevres and Vincennes porcelain.

Blue and white Ceramics decorated with cobalt blue enamel.

Bocage Encrustations of flowers, grass and moss generally used to decorate the supporting plinths of ceramic figures.

Body The material from which a piece of pottery or porcelain is made (the word paste is also used for porcelain).

Bonbonniere Small, lidded novelty box or bowl for sweets.

Bone ash Powder derived from burnt, ground animal bone that was added to porcelain in England in the mid-18th century.

Bone china Type of porcelain incorporating dried bone developed by Josiah Spode and others c.1794, that became the most popular type of English porcelain.

Bracket lobes Flat-topped projecting motif used as a moulding on plates and other tablewares.

Cachepot Holder for a flower pot, similar but smaller than a Jardinière.

Caillouté Term derived from the French word for "pebble", meaning gilding applied in a series of dotted patterns.

Camaieu Monochrome painted decoration resembling ancient shell cameos.

Campana vase Vase shape derived from ancient prototypes resembling an inverted bell.

Caneware Stoneware of pale buff colour fashionable in the late 18th and early 19th century.

Canton porcelain Elaborately decorated and gilded chinese wares produced in the Canton (Guangzhou) district for export to the West.

Cartouche Decorative frame usually surrounding an inscription or pictorial decoration.

Caudle cup Vessel used for drinking caudle – a type of spiced porridge.

Celadon Semi-opaque glaze usually of greenish colour applied to Chinese stoneware.

Charger A large circular or oval dish or plate, usually richly decorated.

China clay A fine white clay also known as kaolin, which is mixed with petuntse to form true hard paste porcelain.

Chinoiserie European interpretation of oriental style decoration, which became particularly fashionable in the 17th and 18th century.

Cobalt blue Mineral used to create blue and white decoration.

Crabstock Spouts and handles modelled as knotted trees and branches, a popular form in the 18th century.

Crackle/crazing Fine network of cracks seen in certain types of glazed surfaces, sometimes used as a deliberate decorative effect, or as a result of ageing.

Creamware Refined lead glazed pottery of a pale colour popular in the 18th century.

Delftware Tin glazed earthenware made in England (delftware) or Holland (Delftware).

Deutsche Blumen Naturalistically painted flowers derived from prints used as a popular decorative motif on 18th century pottery and porcelain.

Dingyao Creamy white type of Chinese porcelain made in the Song dynasty.

Enamel Colours made from glass which fuse with the glaze during firing.

Enghalskrug Type of narrow necked jug with bulbous body popular in Germany and Holland from the mid-17th to the mid-18th century.

Faience Tin-glazed earthenware produced in France or Germany (similar to maiolica).

Famille rose Chinese porcelain decorated with a distinctive palette of opaque enamels.

Famille verte Chinese porcelain decorated with a

distinctive palette of predominantly green translucent enamels.

Flat backs Figurative pottery groups with undetailed almost flat backs, intended to stand on a mantelpiece, they were produced mainly in Staffordshire from c.1840.

Fritware Islamic pottery wares made from silica-rich clay that created a semi translucent body.

Garniture A set of three or more vases of matching and complimentary form intended to stand on a mantelpiece or on the top of a cabinet.

Gilding The use of gold to create decorative effect. Gilding can be applied in a variety of ways: mixed with honey or mercury and fired or applied after firing.

Glaze Glassy coating applied onto the biscuit body of pottery and porcelain and fired to make it non- porous.

Ground Background area of a single colour onto which further enamelled decoration or gilding may be applied.

Hard-paste porcelain Type of porcelain body made using kaolin and petuntse, first developed in China.

Hausmaler Term used to describe an independent painter of German porcelain blanks (most often with reference to Meissen).

Hookah Middle eastern smoking pipe, also known as a Narghili or Kendi.

Imari Japanese porcelain made in the Arita region and exported through the port of Imari. The term refers to pieces decorated with designs probably inspired by brocade textiles, predominately with underglaze blue, iron red and lavish gilding.

Impressed Term generally used to describe a mark or decoration that is stamped or indented into the surface of pottery.

Incised Term generally used to describe a mark or decoration that is cut or scratched into the surface.

Ironstone Hard white earthenware popular from the early 19th century for dinner services and other ornamental and architectural pieces.

Istoriato Mythological, historical or biblical subjects used to decorate the surface of plates, dishes and other maiolica wares from 16thC onward in Italy.

Jasper ware Type of unglazed stoneware body popularized by Josiah Wedgwood.

Jewelled decoration Method of decoration created by drops of enamel over gilding, resembling jewels, popular in France in the 18th century and at Royal Worcester.

Kakiemon Sparse asymmetrical style of decoration on a white ground introduced by Japanese potters in the 17th century.

Kendi Term used for a bulbous drinking vessel, used originally to hold holy water, but also as a hubble-bubble (see Hookah).

Knop Term used to describe the decorative finial on teapot and vase lids.

Kraak-porselein Late Ming Chinese blue and white porcelain exported by Dutch traders to Europe.

Lustre ware Pottery decorated with metallic pigments, popular in the Middle East, and Europe.

Majolica Colourful type of earthenware loosely based on Italian maiolica, popular in Europe and America from c.1850.

Manganese Mineral used to make purple brown pigments.

Overglaze Decoration applied on top of the glaze.

Palette Selection of colours used in decoration.

Parian Unglazed glassy type of porcelain popular for making imitation marble sculpted figures in the 19th century.

Pâte sur pâte Decorative technique made by building up layers of slip on a contrasting ground to simulate the effect of a cameo.

Press moulding Method of producing ceramic objects by forcing clay into a mould.

Salt glaze Glaze used on some stoneware made by throwing salt into the kiln during firing first developed in the Rhineland.

Satsuma Type of Japanese pottery with elaborate decoration, crackle glaze and heavy gilding named after the Japanese port where it was made.

Soft-paste porcelain Type of body developed in Europe in the 16th century made from various materials which may include kaolin, glass, soapstone or bone ash, in an attempt to create true hard-paste porcelain.

Slip Mixture of clay and water used as a form of decoration on some types of pottery.

Spur marks Indentations left in the glaze caused by small stilts used to support an object during firing.

Stoneware Non porous ceramic body made from clay and sand or flint, fired at high temperature.

Tin glaze Opaque white glaze made from tin oxide, used on maiolica, faience and delftware pottery.

Terracotta Red-coloured earthenware pottery, usually unglazed.

Toby jug Tankard or jug in the form of a toper.

Transfer printing Printed decoration made by transferring a design created on a copper plate via transfer paper onto a pottery or porcelain body.

Underglaze Decoration applied to a body before glazing and final firing.

Yue ware Distinctive type of Chinese stoneware coated in green glaze made from the Han dynasty to 10th century.

INDEX

ACKNOWLEDGMENTS

The publishers would like to thank all those who provided pictures for this book and in particular Christie's Images, Letitia Roberts, Director of the Porcelain Department at Sotheby's, for the pictures on pp154 and 155bl, and John Hays, Director of the Americana Department at Christie's for the pictures on pp160c and 160br.

Front cover: **tl** CI; **tr** RIB/CH/P; **cr** SL; bl RIB/CH/P; **br** SL. Back cover CI. Front flap RIB/SL Back flap RIB

2tl&tr RIB/SL; **2cl,c&cr** SPLL; **2bl&br** CI; **3tl** RIB/SL; **3tr** CI; **3c** RIB/SL; **3bl** P; **3br** RIB/SL; **11** SPLL; **15** DS; **16** RIB/JH; **17** RIB/JH; **18** RIB/JM/DS; **19** CL; **20** RIB/JH; **22** AM; **25** SZ; **26t** Be; **26b** CL; **27** SL; **28** B; **29t** RIB/CH/P; **29b** SL; **30** SL; **31** RIB/CH/P; **32** RIB/JM; **33** P; **34** RIB/CH/P; **35b** RIB/CH/P; **35tl** SL; **35tr** RIB/CH/P; **36l** SPLL; **36r** RIB/CH/P; **37t&c** SL; **37b** SPLL; **38t&b** SL; **39t,bl&br** SL; **40l&r** SL; **41t** SPLL; **41bl** SL; **41br** SPLL; **42l** SL; **42r** RIB/CH/P; **43l&r** RIB/CH/P; **43b** SNY; **44l&r** SL; **45t,bl&br** SL; **46t** Be; **46b** CI; **47l&tr** SPLL; **47br** RIB/PB; **48** SPLL; **49tr** RIB/CH/P; **49cr** SL; **49tl** SPLL; **49bl** RIB/CH/P; **50** RIB/CNY; **51tl** RIB/SL; **51tr** CI; **51bl** RIB/SL; **51br** RIB/SL/IB; **52l** RIB/CH/P; **52tr** CI; **52br** RIB/CH/P; **53&b** CI; **54l** CI; **54r** SPLL; **55l** CI; **55tr** SPLL; **55br** CI; **56l** CI; **56r** SL; **57tl&bl** CI; **57r** SL; **58tl,tr&b** RIB/CH/P; **59tl,tr,c&b** CI; **60** RIB/CH/P; **61tl&tr** CI; **61b** SL; **62l** SL; **62tr** CI; **62br** SL; **63t&b** SL; **64t&b** CI; **65l** P; **65tr,bc&br** CI; **66l&r** CI; **67t** RIB/CH/P; **67b** CI; **68t** RIB/CH/P; **68bl** CI; **68br** CI; **69t,bl** CI&br CI; **70l** P; **70b** CI; **71c** RIB/SL; **71b** CI; **72** P; **73tl** P; **73bl&r** RIB/SL; **74l** CI; **74tr** JJM; **74b** CI; **75l** RIB/CH/P; **75tc** P; **75br** CI; **76l** CI; **76r** JHA; **77t&r** Be; **77bl** CI; **78t** P; **78b** RIB/CH/P; **79t** P; **79b** RIB/CH/P; **80l** RIB/CH/P; **80br** P; **81l,tr&br** RIB/CH/P; **82tl** Be; **82tr&b** RIB/CH/P); **83l&r** P; **84l,tr&br** P; **85tl,tr&b** P; **86l** P; **86b** RIB/CH/P; **87l** Be; **87tr&br** RIB/CH/P; **88** CI; **89l&tr** RIB/CH/P; **90l,tr,&br** CI; **91tl** SL; **91bl** SPLL; **91r** CI; **92l&r** CI; **93l** CI; **93r** RIB/CH/P; **94t&b** CI; **95t** SPLL; **95bl&br** CI; **96l&r** CI; **97tl** SPLL; **97tr&b** CI; **98t&b** CI; **99tl,bl&r** CI; **100l&r** CI; **101t&l** CI; **102l** CI; **102r** SPLL; **103bl** CI; **103tl** SPLL; **103r** CI; **104l&r** CI; **105tl** CI; **105bl** SPLL; **105r** CI; **106t&b** CI; **107t&b** CI; **108** C; **109t** CI; **109l** SL; **109r** Be; **110tl,tr&br** CI; **111t&b** CI; **112** CI; **113l** RIB/CH/P; **113tr** CI; **113rc** RIB/CH/P; **113rb** RIB/CH/P; **113b** CI; **114l&r** CI; **115l,tr&br** CI; **116t&b** RIB/CH/P; **117tl** RIB/CH/P; **117bl** CI; **117r** CI; **118l&r** RIB/CH/P; **119tl** Be; **119c,bl&br** CI; **120l&r** CI; **121tl** CI; **121bl** SL; **121r** SPLL; **122t** P; **122b** RIB/CH/P; **123tl** P; **123bl** CI; **123r** RIB/CH/P; **124l** RIB/CH/P; **124c** P; **124r** RIB/CH/P; **125l&tr** RIB/CH/P; **125br** CI; **126l** RIB/CH/P; **126r** P; **127l** P; **127t** RIB/CH/P; **128** P; **129t** CI; **129l** RIB/CH/P; **129r** RIB/CH/P; **130tl** P; **130tr** Be; **130b** CI; **131tl** P; **131bl&r** CI; **132tl** RIB/CH/P; **132bl** CI; **132r** RIB/CH/P; **133t** RIB/CH/P; **133b** CI; **134l** RIB/CH/P; **134r** CI; **135tl,bl&r** CI; **136** P; **137t,cl&bl** P; **137r** RIB/CH/P; **138tl** P; **138bl** RIB/CH/P; **138r** P; **139l** RIB/DL;

139tr RIB/CH/P; **139br** P; **140tl** RIB/B; **140tr** RIB/CH/P; **140bl** RIB/IB; **140br** RIB/B; **141t&b** GCC; **142t** SL; **142b** Be; **143t,bl&r** P; **144l,c&r** P; **145l&r** RIB/CH/P; **146l** SL; **146r** RIB/CH/P; **147tl** RIB/CH/P; **147rc** B; **147r** RDP; **148t&bl** CSK; **148br** RIB/CH/P; **149t&c** RIB/CH/P; **149b** Be; **150l,tc&r** P; **151tl** MJ; **151tr** RIB/CH/P; **151b** P; **152r** RIB/CH/P; **152tl&bl** P; **153tl&bl** B; **153r** RIB/CH/P; **154** SL; **155tl** GDS; **155bl** SL; **155br** GDS; **156t&b** DR; **157t** DR; **157c** CL; **157b** DR; **158l,c&r** DR; **159t&b** DR; **1** 160c CL; **160bl** GDS; **160br** CL; **161tl** RT; **161tr,c&b** WTK

KEY

b bottom, **c** centre, **l** left, **r** right, **t** top

AM Allyson McDermott
B Bonhams, London
Be Bearnes, Torquay
CI Christie's Images, London
CL Christie's London
CNY Christie's New York
CSK Christie's South Kensington
DL Dr Laird
DR David Rago
DS D Stratton
DSe Dennis Severs
GCC Goss & Crested China Ltd
GDS Gary & Diana Stradling
IB Ian Booth
JH Jacqui Hurst
JHA Jonathan Home Antiques
JJM J & J May/John May
JM James Merrell
MJ Malcolm Jennings
P Phillips, London
PB Patricia Bayer
RDP Richard Dennis Publications (Plate XLVIII "Wedgwood Ceramics" by Maureen Batkin published by Richard Dennis
RIB Reed International Books Ltd
RIB/CH/P Reed International Books Ltd./Chris Halton/Phillips
RT Robert Teitelman
SL Sotheby's London
SPLL Sotheby's Picture Library, London
SNY Sotheby's New York
SZ Sotheby's Zurich
WTK William and Teresa Kurau

THE PENTECOSTAL EXPERIENCE

The
Pentecostal Experience

by

J. Massingberd Ford

PAULIST PRESS

Paramus, N. J.   New York, N. Y.

I
The Spirit
in History

The First Creation

"Pentecost" has always been in the mind of God. The second chapter of Genesis presents us with a parable. God created man out of the clods of the earth and then breathed into him the breath of life. Jesus' own tradition—the Jewish tradition—understood this as a symbol of the inspiration of the Holy Spirit into mankind so that human beings could live in intimate communion with God. They could experience a vital sense of God's presence through spiritual senses such as sight, hearing and touch, and they could love God for himself rather than his gifts. In distinction from the animals they possessed the gift of speech with which they could praise and bless God and commune with one another.

Sin for Jews was seen as a quenching of the Spirit. In its wake it produced dullness of the spiritual senses, lethargy in regard to prayer (that is, communion with God), and an indifference to God's presence. The Holy Spirit was seen as a delicate, well-mannered guest who left man complete freedom of will and who awaited an invitation from him, very often a warm invitation, before entering into communion with him. Certain prophets, prophetesses, and leaders in the Old Testament did proffer this invitation, and consequently they were filled with charismatic gifts. We can think, for example, of

3

Elijah, Elisha and, most of all, Moses. Sin remains a refusal to issue this invitation, and the Holy Spirit rarely comes unasked.

The Second Creation

Perhaps the person to offer the warmest invitation to the Holy Spirit was Mary, the mother of Jesus. She said, quite simply, "Behold the handmaid of the Lord, be done unto me according to your word." This was an irresistible invitation, and the Holy Spirit came with all his power, taking her humanity and creating of it Jesus, the Son of God. Catholics speak about the "Immaculate Heart of Mary." When they do so, they are not referring to absence of sexual sin or sexual desire in Mary; rather they use the word "immaculate" as scripture uses the word "unblemished" for the lambs which were offered to God. If a lamb was without blemish, it had no handicap and was full of vitality. In the same way, Mary's heart was poised with expectant love and exuberant hope for the fullfillment of God's promise to his people, and she was not disappointed.

But Mary's vocation could not have been a continuous honeymoon with her spouse, the Holy Spirit. Her unique vocation and the unique vocation of her son, together with their hypersensitivity in regard to the fulfillment of God's will and their abhorrence of sin, must have brought suffering and isolation upon them which remains unparalleled in the history of mankind. Yet, the Holy Spirit seems

4

to have given them a unique kind of fortitude and wisdom, a sense of humor and trust. Surely, the mother of the Son of God followed the example of the mother mentioned in 2 Maccabees 7 and combined a woman's reason with manly courage, and it may be that she lightened Jesus' cross by meeting him with a radiant, encouraging smile rather than tears on his way to Calvary. We must regard 1 Corinthians 13 as a picture not only of Jesus, but also of Mary. This chapter describes what we mean by the Immaculate Heart of Mary. When Mary gave this ready consent, God once again breathed the Spirit of life into mankind and Jesus was conceived within her. It was no wonder that Mary broke into prophetic utterance in her song, the Magnificat.

Jesus, the Bearer of the Spirit

The little boy Jesus grew to youth and manhood, but the Holy Spirit did not reveal much of this period of his life in holy scripture. It was one of hidden growth known only by its fruits: his relationship with his Father, his charismatic service toward mankind, and his giving of the Spirit on the cross. Only St. Luke tells us of the finding of the child Jesus in the temple, and here he stresses Jesus' wisdom and understanding rather than his miraculous power. Yet we must not think of these hidden years as unproductive. They were like the grain of mustard seed which became a tree and under which all could find shelter.

5

Jesus' public ministry in which these fruits were manifest lasted a short time, probably a year, certainly not longer than two years and a few months. The signal from the Heavenly Father for Jesus to begin his public apostolic life came with his baptism. Jesus approached John the Baptist as an individual without sin, full of the Holy Spirit of God. The purpose of the baptism seems to have been the release of the spiritual powers which Jesus already possessed.

Jesus' temptation reveals the opposition of Satan and possibly the temptation to abuse his powers. For example, Jesus appears to have been tempted by personal ambition, desire for wealth, desire to behave in a sensational way, to succumb to worshiping Satan, to achieve material and political advantages. Jesus realized that the hundredfold blessing which the servants of God can expect from their Heavenly Father must not be sought in the wrong way. He overcame all these temptations and began his public ministry.

The Public Ministry of Jesus

In his public ministry, Jesus showed the use of nearly all the ministries listed by St. Paul in 1 Corinthians 12, 4–11. The only gifts which he does not seem to have used are the gift of tongues and interpretation. The heart of the charismatic ministry lay in the restoring of the relationship of each individual to the Heavenly Father. Hence, Jesus summed up his ministry in the prayer which he taught to his disciples—the Our Father. The best commentary on the Our Father is Jesus' own life, death and resurrection. In this prayer there is no explicit request for miracles such as healing. Indeed Jesus appears to have portrayed miracle-working as preliminary to the essential charismatic ministry. He saw miracles as signs, but signs which pointed beyond themselves. He reproached those who came merely for this ministry, and he required loving faith in himself as a criterion of a true disciple. He also warned his disciples that even miracles such as resurrection from the dead would not cause people to believe (Luke 16, 19–31).

Most of the miracles Jesus performed occurred in the beginning of his public life. They are far overshadowed by the end of his life, which revealed the glory of his suffering and the splendor of his resurrection. The gift of prophecy also seemed to be used more toward the end of his life (e.g., Mark 13 and 14). After his resurrection, he appears to have concentrated on a teaching ministry on behalf of his disciples.

The early Christians did not distinguish as sharply as we do between the resurrection, the ascension, and Pentecost. For example, St. John indicates that Jesus passed on the Spirit from the cross and then gave the Holy Spirit formally to the disciples on Easter. St. Luke, however, indicates that the Holy Spirit came with all his power on the Jewish feast of

7

Pentecost, about ten days after Easter. What was important to the early Christians was the death, resurrection and giving of the Spirit, rather than their precise sequence.

Pentecost

Pentecost (Acts 2) is an event parallel to the annunciation and to Jesus' baptism. During the earthly life of Jesus, Mary and the apostles, like Jesus in his hidden years, grew in their relationship to the Father through Jesus. Perhaps many received baptism of water and the Spirit. Pentecost for them was the signal to release those gifts which they had received from Jesus for the glory of God and the good of mankind. It was like the baptism of Jesus. It was also a new birth.

As an outward sign of this new birth, God gave a mysterious prayer gift, the gift of tongues. Just as God had given Adam the gift of speech, thereby distinguishing him from animals, so he gave a new gift of speech on the feast of Pentecost. Adam had misused his speech, and by this misuse he had demoralized and debilitated himself and his brothers. St. James shows this demoralizing power of the abuse of speech in Chapter 3 of his epistle. The gift of tongues is a direct contrast, for it counterbalances the abuse of speech. It is a new language or languages not learned in a human way: a prayer gift used for the building up of the individual and indirectly for the community. The essence of the gift of tongues is one's surrender to God; very often during its use one has a lively experience of the presence of God. It is certainly a useful gift, but a means to an end, not an end in itself. One is perfectly in control of oneself and can begin and cease to speak at will.

But the gift of tongues was not the only gift which God gave on Pentecost. The men and women who emerged from the upper room did so as new individuals with new powers—indeed, all the powers which Jesus had used in his ministry. The Church was and is the true, resurrected, community body of Christ, and as such each individual receives a responsibility to fulfill—he is to show forth and relive a certain part of Christ's life. Christ, as perfect God and perfect man, could perform all the ministries of the Spirit as an individual, but Christian men and women perform them together as a community, thus showing forth Christ. St. Luke, who wrote both his Gospel and Acts, makes a very close parallel between the events in the life of Jesus and those of the early Church.

However we must notice that the title of St. Luke's second work is "Acts of Apostles," not "*The* Acts of *the* Apostles." Acts is meant to be a protocol for the normal life of the Church, just as the Gospels show Christ who is to be imitated by each of his followers.

Has the Church Reflected Acts?

Has the Church been faithful to this protocol?

Both structure and charism are necessary for the Church. Acts and Corinthians show more of the charismatic character of the Church and the epistles to Timothy and Titus show the necessity of the structure. Both are inspired by the same Spirit. Both structure and charism can go to extremes. So it is that the Church in her struggle to keep the balance shows a constant vacillation between these two extremes.

One of the first extremes was a schism called Montanism, which began as a perfectly orthodox charismatic section of the Church, but made many serious mistakes as time went on. The members came to look upon themselves as a kind of elite, calling themselves spiritual people and regarding the other Catholics as sensual people. There was a pitiful and arrogant exclusiveness about their community. They over-stressed the charisms, especially prophecy, and made some of their writings equal to scripture. They inculcated new asceticisms, especially fasting, and they set up their own charismatic leaders and their own hierarchy. They broke up family life and had strange views about the second coming of Christ. Further, many of their prophets were false and gave way to sinful lives of avarice and impurity.

There were other charismatic movements within the structure of the Church which were perfectly legitimate. These arose around men and women who had emerged from their "hidden years" to the full flowering of their apostolate in Christ. These people

10

used the gifts which they had received in the sacraments of baptism, confirmation and the eucharist, and eventually they experienced what Catholics call "a second conversion" or "a release of the spirit" and a desire to give oneself completely to God. Such, for example, were the martyrs, who joined themselves in a special way to the passion of Christ. Others were called to integrate their spiritual life and their intellectual life—for example, the great St. Augustine of Hippo, St. Bernard of Clairvaux, St. Thomas Aquinas and St. Dominic. In a special manner they united themselves to the teaching aspect of Jesus' life. Others were organizers of charismatic contemplative communities, such as St. Benedict and St. Francis of Assisi. Others were social workers such as St. John Bosco. Others had individual apostolates. Most notable of all is St. Catherine of Siena.

An Example in Catherine

Catherine represents an individual in whom the ministries of the Spirit listed by St. Paul (in 1 Cor. 12, 4–12) were fully realized. Let us recall these gifts:

"To each is given the manifestation of the Spirit for the common good. To one is given through the Spirit the utterance of wisdom, and to the other the utterance of knowledge according to the same Spirit, to another faith by the same Spirit, to another gifts of healing by the one Spirit, to another the working of miracles, to another prophecy, to another

11

the ability to distinguish between spirits, to another various kinds of tongues, to another the interpretation of tongues" (1 Cor. 12, 7–10).

Although we cannot repudiate the fact that Catherine must have been a shrewd and intelligent young woman, surely she possessed the utterance of wisdom and knowledge. On several occasions professional theologians came to interview her, hoping to catch her upon some theological point, especially misinterpretation of scripture, but they always went away impressed with her wisdom and understanding. More than once she seems to have shown the gift of inspired preaching. Once, for example, she was invited to speak to some monks, and afterward the superior declared that she had touched upon every need of each individual monk without previous knowledge of the condition of the religious community. She had the gift of faith in abundance; at her faithful prayer God would perform many miracles, both spiritual and physical. She is reported to have performed quite a number of healings—for example, the healing of her confessor from plague—as well as the multiplication of wine in a wine vat. She was a prophetess both in the sense of one who was given the gift of prediction (she once predicted the great schism in the Church when an anti-pope was elected) and also in the sense of one who spoke forth words inspired by God. The *Dialogue* dictated to her secretaries while she was in ecstasy may be regarded as prophecy in this last sense of the word.

This contains teaching on divine providence, discretion, prayer, and obedience.

Catherine could distinguish between good and evil spirits, for she could sense when a person had turned from God or was possessed by evil spirits or when he had a special potentiality to serve God. We do not know whether she possessed the gift of tongues—that is, the ability to speak a language not learned in a human way—but it is reported that she learned to understand the Latin office quite suddenly, even though one must remember that Latin is not difficult for an Italian to master.

In 1968 Catherine was proclaimed as a Doctor of the Church. She is rightly called Doctor for her teaching which she gave as an outstanding director of souls, for her erudition in her *Dialogue on Divine Providence,* and not least for her wise and dynamic dissertation to prelates in the Church. On one occasion she was invited to speak before the pope and cardinals—a privilege denied to women at Vatican Council II. Her special teaching was on the highest gift of the Holy Spirit, the gift of love. Let us cite a few examples. "Man is like a candle to be lighted— to be lighted in God. The combustible material is love." "Your material is love because I have created you for love; hence without love you cannot live." "Without love one must die: a lamp without oil goes out." This light of love is kindled each day by the eucharist which is the source of love. To love is to insert oneself in the nature of God.

13

She also taught a great devotion to the blood of Christ—perhaps we should say the "lifeblood" of Christ—which she likened to fire. For example she spoke of "the blood sprinkled in the fire of love; there is no blood without fire, and no fire without blood. In the sprinkling of blood we perceive the burning fire of love." She speaks of the "life blood" of Jesus as that which animates us, warms us, enlivens and enlightens us. It gives light, energy, color and beauty to the Mystical Body of Christ, the Church, and turns us from the pallor of death to the joy of vivacious life in Christ by his "roseate" blood. The foundation of her spiritual life was the reception of the blessed eucharist which she was sometimes permitted to receive daily, a great exception in her day. For her, reception of holy communion was the interchange of souls, the flowing of the life of Jesus into her own soul, and after the reception of the eucharist she frequently fell into ecstasy in which she received enlightenment for the apostolic work which awaited her after communion.

We may also note that Catherine had a great devotion to the sacrament of penance. For her this was not a mere recitation of sin but a recital of the graces which God had given her in prayer and, in the light of this, her own sinfulness. She had an intimate but most spiritual and pure natural relationship with her confessors, especially Blessed Raymond of Capua. This might be a model for us nowadays.

The Church has deeply appreciated the contribution of these charismatic leaders to the life of the Body of Christ. The Church has held them up for our example, instructing us that the Church, the Body of Christ, transcends space and time, and that we can communicate with those people whose lives are "changed, but not taken away." The Church has given her blessing to our veneration of these charismatic leaders, and by canonization she has, as it were, declared that they were "filled with the Spirit."

Acts of Apostles in the 19th and 20th Centuries

There charismatic leaders might appear as merely historical figures for us, and we must ask whether the Church in the 20th century continues to reflect Acts of Apostles. In the late 19th century, the vicar of Christ, Leo XIII, wrote three important letters which he circulated to the whole Church. One was on the dignity of the individual, another on the importance of biblical studies, and a third on the Holy Spirit. Leo XIII was preparing the way not only for special charismatic leaders, but for a charismatic-hierarchical Church which would send forth apostles to the whole world to help renew civil and domestic life and to assist in the ecumenical mission of the Church. Leo XIII stressed devotion to Mary and to the Holy Spirit, asking members of the Church to pray for nine days before the feast of Pentecost each year. He stressed that there is only a difference of *degree* between the historical charismatic leaders and every member of the Church. We all have the same gifts but we do not always use them in the most economical and dynamic way.

Not long after Leo XIII's letter, non-Roman Catholic Christians began to pray for unity; very soon thereafter Catholics followed their example. From the early part of the 20th century there were sporadic charismatic "happenings," miraculous conversions of individuals, and sometimes conversions of great crowds of people to Christ. Great healers arose. There were prophecies and visions, and many people received the gift of tongues. These people called these charismatic "happenings" the "baptism in the Spirit." At first, these events occurred mainly among the less educated classes. But these were merely outward signs of inner reality, like the miracles of Jesus. It is as if they were intended to catch people's attention, to lead them to something greater: faith in Jesus. They were very similar to the experiences of many Catholics, especially the charismatic leaders to whom we have referred. But, as is well known, the Catholic Church has always been cautious about religious experience and has taught Catholics not to talk about these experiences, whereas non-Catholics are used to "giving testimony." Thus it seemed to non-Roman Catholics that there were no charisms within the Catholic Church. This was a mistaken idea. There were many charisms, but there was no "news release," as one might say.

However, in the 20th century, God raised up a great prophet in the Roman Catholic Church. This was John XXIII, the vicar of Christ. He had a prophetic insight and it is said that he received some visions (although we do not know this for certain). However, he did have the gifts of wisdom and counsel and, richest of all, the gift of love. He organized a general Council for the Catholic Church and asked the members of the Church to prepare for this by praying very fervently. He composed a prayer and deliberately asked God to send a new Pentecost. God answered this prayer. Pentecost came in various ways, accompanied by suffering, temptations, defections, and victories over temptations. The documents produced from the general Council are witness to the charisms of wisdom, counsel and love.

However, Pentecost also came in a more dramatic and overt fashion, as we shall see.

II

The Spirit
in Today's Church

The Catholic Experience

Since approximately 1962, Roman Catholics over the United States have been experiencing what other Christians call "the baptism in the Spirit," or "the baptism of the Spirit." What exactly does this mean? Among many non-Roman Catholic Christians, it means that the individual experiences the personal presence of God, usually Jesus Christ, and perhaps also the mysterious prayer gift, the gift of tongues—speaking to God in a language which has not been learned in a human way but is suddenly "given." Frequently, the use of this prayer gift enables a person to experience the wonderful presence of God. People who receive these privileges are led to commit their lives to Jesus in a very generous and courageous way and most of them persevere in prayer and apostolic work.

Naturally, throughout the ages, this kind of experience has been and is well known to Catholics, but no one spoke about it very often. One major difference between the view of Catholics and that of other Christians is that this "baptism of the Spirit" does not necessarily entail the prayer gift, the gift of tongues. However, "tongues" are mentioned by St. Bernard, St. Alphonsus Liguori, St. John of the Cross, St. Teresa of Avila, and others.

21

In Catholic terminology, perhaps we should say that this experience is a touch—but not the state—of infused contemplation. When one experiences God as a living reality, draws close to him in prayer, and determines to make generous sacrifices for him, this is "the baptism of the Spirit." Sometimes people call this the "second conversion," a turning toward God in a fuller way, an establishment of an I-Thou relationship. If one takes advantage of these graces from God, very often one experiences more gifts of prayer, including some of the charismatic gifts which St. Paul mentions in 1 Corinthians 12 and elsewhere.

These experiences are described by the great spiritual writers, such as St. Teresa of Avila, St. John of the Cross and St. Francis de Sales. They are usually the outcome of a life dedicated to God through prayer and loving service to others. Sometimes this experience comes to those who are not exactly committed to God or even people who do not know God or who have turned away from him. This is rather a special event, yet it has occurred more and more frequently during these recent years. There have been cases of almost miraculous conversions, that is, first conversions to Our Lord, and numerous cases of second conversion. Both types of experience have frequently been accompanied by the mysterious gift of tongues.

So nowadays when Catholics say they have received the "baptism of the Spirit" they are saying that they have experienced God in a truly living way.

22

Old Testament and seven listed in the Greek Ol
Testament.)

How can a Christian pursue these higher gifts? I
is only by the closest possible union with the Give
and this is found principally in the sacraments an
in mental prayer, accompanied by deeds of lovin
kindness to our fellow men and women. First of al
we must have a deep appreciation of the sacramen
of baptism and confirmation which find their fulfil
ment in the eucharist. We can express this best b
following the Church's liturgy and—as we wer
aptized into Christ and confirmed into his Hol
irit—following the liturgical cycle which relate
birth, baptism, life, death and resurrection an
nsion of Jesus, and the Pentecost cycle. Thes
ical celebrations are no mere historical com
rations but are a dynamic and efficacious wa
ing ourselves to particular aspects of th
of Christ and his Church. They culminat
ster vigil, when every Christian renews hi
aptismal vows, and they find their fu
n the feast of Pentecost, when the Hol
released in those in Jerusalem. In th
le we concentrate on the Giver rathe
and this is very good, indeed.

3–58, Jesus says: ". . . truly, truly
s you eat the flesh of the Son o
s blood, you have no life in you

This is usually accompanied by a great love for Holy Scripture, a deep appreciation of the fatherhood of God and sometimes of the motherhood of Our Lady, a love for the eucharist and the sacraments, an apostolic zeal but one which is not immoderate in nature, and, above all, a great hunger for prayer.

Sometimes the experience is received alone, very often before the blessed sacrament, but also it has often been received through an individual's friends gathering around him or her, placing their hands upon his head and praying with faith that there will be a release of the Holy Spirit. The novelty of this situation lies in the number, age and status of those affected and in the more frequent bestowal of the gift of tongues. What had taken place after years of discipline and practice has sometimes appeared to be well nigh instantaneous, and people who were living an active life now appear to be able to combine an almost contemplative life and the active life. It may be, that in this age of skepticism when so many people are denying the existence of God or turning to humanism, God has not disregarded the sincerity which may be in their hearts, even though they have been led to extremes, and God has given them this special blessing so they may realize that there are "more things in heaven and earth, Horatio, than are dreamt of in your philosophy."

Dangers and Obedience

This is indeed a great blessing. But there are

dangers attached to this privilege. The recipients have not arrived at the contemplative state, and indeed many may not be called to do so. But God has given them a taste of contemplative prayer, and this taste should urge them to pursue a more generous, orderly, yet flexible spiritual life, if possible under the guidance of an experienced counsellor—either a priest, a sister, a layman or laywoman.

One must ever bear in mind that, in distinction to the sacrament of baptism, this release (baptism) of the Spirit is not a permanent state and does not give an indelible character to the individual. It is a gratuitous gift and it may go as quickly as God gives it. When it comes to those who have little practice in spiritual life, it may cause them to be thrown off their feet, as it were, with the joy and beauty and grandeur of the experience. They may go to extremes or misinterpret certain things which happen in their own prayer or prophecies, or words of wisdom and knowledge which they hear in their prayer group. It is therefore very necessary to realize that one's own judgment is not sufficient when one reaches a prayer experience which is not attained by human effort. Just as after Jesus' baptism, the devil, personal ambition, and other forces assailed Our Lord, so the trials are bound to come to his disciples.

It is here that we find a place for spiritual obedience or hearing. Nowadays many people decry obedience to superiors, and they are justified in a certain assertion of their personal maturity and education which God has been pleased to give them. However, it would seem that the origin of obedience lies in the realm of the higher spiritual gifts. Here, human maturity is not sufficient, and the individual to whom God has graciously given these gifts is the mercy of his or her own delusion by imagin⸻ or, perhaps, evil spirits, if the subject do⸻ humbly submit to another spiritual and re⸻ person and to the guidance of the Chur⸻

The Roman Catholic Church has s⸻ example of prudence and wisdom i⸻ ceptance of miraculous occurrence⸻ matic gifts. We may quote, for⸻ Fatima, Teresa Neumann, and⸻ but a few. No charismatic C⸻ tury is greater than the c⸻ Catholic Church throug⸻ be humble enough to ⸻ tested.

The Higher Gif⸻

We have s⸻ miracle wor⸻ thing grea⸻ gifts whi⸻ also t⸻ eloq⸻ unde⸻ fear of t⸻

He who eats my flesh and drinks my blood has eternal life and I will raise him up until the last day. For my flesh is food indeed and my blood is drink indeed. He who eats my flesh and drinks my blood abides in me and I in him. As the living Father sent me and I live because of the Father, so he who eats me will live because of me. This is the bread which came down from heaven, not such as the fathers ate and died. He who eats this bread will live forever."

Charismatic Catholics must take these words deeply to heart. It is in the blessed eucharist, as this text shows, that we have the closest union, not only with Jesus but also with the Father and the Holy Spirit. Indeed, in the early Church, Christians saw everything, especially baptism and confirmation, leading up the eucharist, which was and still is regarded as the totality of the Christian experience. In sacramental baptism we enter into the messianic kingdom and into the missionary work of Jesus and his Church; in the eucharist we are invited to the messianic banquet wherein we share the common principle of spiritual life—preservation through our communion with Jesus.

In this eucharistic banquet, we are in communion not only with all our brothers and sisters in the Church on earth, but also we are brought close to every member of the Church, whether in the intermediate state of purgatory or in the triumphant state of the Church in heaven. Hence we enjoy in the eucharist the companionship of the charismatic leaders of the Catholic Church throughout all ages and the intellectual spirits such as angels. But our communion with others in the eucharist must not distract us from the fact that the primary focus of union is with God. In the sacred eucharist we come into a sublime communion with Jesus in his resurrected state. As we receive Jesus, we receive, we might say, the charismatic Christ. Here is the Giver of all spiritual gifts in his glorious state of resurrection, carrying with him and within him the spiritual gifts of wisdom which he showed in his teaching, of understanding, of counsel, the ministries of the Spirit such as healing and miracle working, and above all, his infinite love for the Father and for us. It is with the most expectant and lively faith that we should make this tryst with Our Lord and Master, the charismatic Christ, and it is at this moment that we should ask for union with the Giver of all gifts and the grace to enable us to carry out apostolic work.

We must note, also, that St. Paul placed great emphasis upon the eucharist. In 1 Corinthians 11, 27–32, St. Paul is very insistent about our attitude toward the eucharist:

"Whoever therefore eats the bread or drinks the cup of the Lord in an unworthy manner will be guilty of profaning the body and blood of the Lord. Let a man examine himself and so eat of the bread and drink of the cup, for anyone who eats and drinks without discerning the body, eats and drinks judgment upon himself. That is why so many of you are weak and ill and some have died. But if we judged ourselves truly we should not be judged. But when we are judged by the Lord, we are chastened so that we may not be condemned along with the world."

St. Paul speaks about the necessity of a most reverent and pure approach to this sacrament, and he indicates that the Corinthians are spiritually weak or lacking in spiritual vitality because they have not approached the eucharist in the right way. It ever behooves us to examine this expectant faith, charity with our brothers and sisters, and the tenor of our whole lives and to approach this sacrament in the right way. It may be noted, also, that St. Paul *may* also indicate that the Corinthians were physically weak or ill because they did not approach the eucharist properly. There have certainly been cases where the reception of the eucharist has brought physical healing. We may also note that most of the charismatic leaders in the Roman Catholic Church had a very deep devotion to the eucharist. Once again, we may think of the example of St. Catherine of Siena.

Spontaneous Prayer Groups

Within the last few years there has been an increasing number of Christians who have formed groups in order to have spontaneous community prayer. These groups comprise Christians from every walk of life—town and gown, student and professor, men and women, religious and lay people, and also people of varying dispositions with regard to "liberal" or "conservative" Catholic thinking. The cause of unity within the group lies in the members' faith in Jesus Christ as a living and vital person who is intimately concerned for each individual. They often enjoy a frequent and acute awareness of his resurrected presence. The desire to join together in such prayer groups should be quite natural to Catholics who have joined together to enjoy the resurrected presence of Jesus in the eucharist, although the eucharistic presence is of a different order from his presence in a prayer group. Many members of these groups have been "baptized in the Spirit." Their experience of the love of the Trinity naturally produces within them a love for their neighbor. Hence, they are drawn together in a community of prayer and love, accompanied by moderate apostolic fervor. For true love of the Father cannot but engender fraternal and sororal charity. True prayer cannot remain totally exclusive, individual and—as many would suggest today—a mere subjective experience.

In other words, a prudent sharing of religious experience is a function of the Mystical Body of Christ, the Church. It was thus that religious communities were born, and it is thus that these prayer communities of priests and laity are also born. This fact is at the heart of St. Paul's teaching. In the center of his teaching on the eucharist and the

Mystical Body of Christ in 1 Corinthians 12–15, he describes early Christian spontaneous prayer and charismatic meetings thus:

"What then, brethren? When you come together, each one has a hymn, a lesson, a revelation, a tongue, or an interpretation. Let all things be done for edification. If any one speak in a tongue, let there be only two or at most three, and each in turn; and let one interpret. But if there be no one to interpret, let each of them keep silence in church and speak to himself and to God. Let two or three prophets speak, and let the others weigh what is said. If a revelation is made to another sitting by, let the first be silent. For you can all prophesy one by one, so that all may learn and all be encouraged; and the spirits of the prophets are subject to prophets. For God is not a God of confusion but of peace" (1 Corinthians 14, 26–33).

Most likely this took place within the eucharistic celebration. We note the elements—hymns, lessons, etc. Our description of the meetings will follow this order. However, by no means is every element present at every meeting; for example there may be many meetings without "revelation" or "prophecy." The meeting is entirely unstructured, but usually there is a "chairman" or "chairwoman."

(1) *Hymns*

Frequently, the meeting commences with a prayer to the Holy Spirit and a hymn, often one of praise. During the meeting, people quite spontaneously begin hymns that they would like to sing, or suggest ones they wish to hear. At some meetings there is guitar accompaniment.

(2) *Bible Reading*

Bible reading is very common. There is a custom of "praying for a text," that is, the reader prays that he or she may be guided to a passage which will be especially pertinent to those attending the meeting. It is remarkable—if anything is remarkable under the guidance of the Holy Spirit—that when this practice is followed by several people at the same meeting a theme is built up; for example, most of the passages read might revolve around love, joy and peace, or all around apostolic works. Then one who feels disposed may add a brief comment or exhortation on the text or offer extempore prayer on a kindred theme.

(3) *Revelation*

A revelation (Greek "apocalypse") may be given when a member receives what Catholics commonly call intellectual or imaginary visions. (In the writer's experience no ocular vision has occurred at the prayer meetings.) An intellectual vision occurs when no image is present to the recipient either to the "eye of the mind" or "to the physical eye," but a Presence is experienced and the recipient of this experience usually knows with great certitude

This is usually accompanied by a great love for Holy Scripture, a deep appreciation of the fatherhood of God and sometimes of the motherhood of Our Lady, a love for the eucharist and the sacraments, an apostolic zeal but one which is not immoderate in nature, and, above all, a great hunger for prayer.

Sometimes the experience is received alone, very often before the blessed sacrament, but also it has often been received through an individual's friends gathering around him or her, placing their hands upon his head and praying with faith that there will be a release of the Holy Spirit. The novelty of this situation lies in the number, age and status of those affected and in the more frequent bestowal of the gift of tongues. What had taken place after years of discipline and practice has sometimes appeared to be well nigh instantaneous, and people who were living an active life now appear to be able to combine an almost contemplative life and the active life. It may be, that in this age of skepticism when so many people are denying the existence of God or turning to humanism, God has not disregarded the sincerity which may be in their hearts, even though they have been led to extremes, and God has given them this special blessing so they may realize that there are "more things in heaven and earth, Horatio, than are dreamt of in your philosophy."

Dangers and Obedience

This is indeed a great blessing. But there are

dangers attached to this privilege. The recipients have not arrived at the contemplative state, and indeed many may not be called to do so. But God has given them a taste of contemplative prayer, and this taste should urge them to pursue a more generous, orderly, yet flexible spiritual life, if possible under the guidance of an experienced counsellor—either a priest, a sister, a layman or laywoman.

One must ever bear in mind that, in distinction to the sacrament of baptism, this release (baptism) of the Spirit is not a permanent state and does not give an indelible character to the individual. It is a gratuitous gift and it may go as quickly as God gives it. When it comes to those who have little practice in spiritual life, it may cause them to be thrown off their feet, as it were, with the joy and beauty and grandeur of the experience. They may go to extremes or misinterpret certain things which happen in their own prayer or prophecies, or words of wisdom and knowledge which they hear in their prayer group. It is therefore very necessary to realize that one's own judgment is not sufficient when one reaches a prayer experience which is not attained by human effort. Just as after Jesus' baptism, the devil, personal ambition, and other forces assailed Our Lord, so the trials are bound to come to his disciples.

It is here that we find a place for spiritual obedience or hearing. Nowadays many people decry obedience to superiors, and they are justified in a certain assertion of their personal maturity and education which God has been pleased to give them. However, it would seem that the origin of obedience lies in the realm of the higher spiritual gifts. Here, human maturity is not sufficient, and the individual to whom God has graciously given these gifts is at the mercy of his or her own delusion by imagination or, perhaps, evil spirits, if the subject does not humbly submit to another spiritual and responsible person and to the guidance of the Church at large.

The Roman Catholic Church has set a splendid example of prudence and wisdom in her tardy acceptance of miraculous occurrences and the charismatic gifts. We may quote, for example, Lourdes, Fatima, Teresa Neumann, and Padre Pio, to name but a few. No charismatic Catholic of the 20th century is greater than the charismatic leaders in the Catholic Church throughout the ages and he should be humble enough to let all spirits, good or bad, be tested.

The Higher Gifts

We have said that the gift of tongues, the gift of miracle working or of healing is a prelude to something greater. This something greater comprises the gifts which Isaiah lists in Chapter 11 (verses 2ff.) and also the gift of love about which St. Paul speaks so eloquently in 1 Corinthians 13. Isaiah lists wisdom, understanding, counsel, might, knowledge, piety, fear of the Lord. (There are six listed in the Hebrew

Old Testament and seven listed in the Greek Old Testament.)

How can a Christian pursue these higher gifts? It is only by the closest possible union with the Giver, and this is found principally in the sacraments and in mental prayer, accompanied by deeds of loving kindness to our fellow men and women. First of all, we must have a deep appreciation of the sacraments of baptism and confirmation which find their fulfillment in the eucharist. We can express this best by following the Church's liturgy and—as we were baptized into Christ and confirmed into his Holy Spirit—following the liturgical cycle which relates the birth, baptism, life, death and resurrection and ascension of Jesus, and the Pentecost cycle. These liturgical celebrations are no mere historical commemorations but are a dynamic and efficacious way of uniting ourselves to particular aspects of the mystery of Christ and his Church. They culminate in the Easter vigil, when every Christian renews his or her baptismal vows, and they find their full flowering in the feast of Pentecost, when the Holy Spirit was released in those in Jerusalem. In the liturgical cycle we concentrate on the Giver rather than the gifts, and this is very good, indeed.

The Eucharist

In John 6, 53–58, Jesus says: "... truly, truly I say to you, unless you eat the flesh of the Son of Man and drink his blood, you have no life in you.

whether this is Jesus, the Blessed Mother, or a saint. Many members experience the presence of Jesus either standing or seated in the center of the circle around which the members group themselves. If this presence really comes from God it produces love, joy and peace and a desire to serve God and one's neighbor.

At other times, but less frequently, a member might receive an "imaginary" vision. This is rather a misleading term; it does not mean "produced by the imagination" but an image seen by the spiritual sight. Catholics normally accept what are known as the "spiritual senses" over and above the natural senses. One example of this type of revelation may suffice. A lady received an image of a narrow straight path at the end of which stood Our Lord; it seemed that as she gazed at Christ the path was flooded with light and she could run swiftly along the path but if she withdrew her eyes from Christ the path was shrouded in darkness. This image or apocalypse urged many people to keep their attention on Christ during the ensuing week.

(4) *A Tongue*

Many—but not all—of those who attend prayer meetings have received what is known as "the gift of tongues." We have spoken of this gift previously. Usually one does not understand the words, but the gist of the prayer is often conveyed. The prayer language is used when one is at a loss to find words to praise God, or when one does not know how to intercede for other people, as a powerful weapon against sin, and to give one joy in the Holy Spirit. Singing in "tongues" is beautiful and soul-restoring. To hear a chorus of people singing in different languages and different tunes—Eastern and Western— and yet to realize that this harmonizes musically is quite astonishing!

The prayer gift of tongues may be used privately (1 Cor. 14, 4. 17) or it may be placed at the service of the community. The latter occurs when one feels a strong urge to speak a sentence or two aloud as a message or exhortation to the group. One prays silently that one may not be misled by one's imagination or by the evil one and, being reasonably satisfied, one speaks forth. The group then prays that God will grant an interpretation or translation. Sometimes one is not given, but usually either the speaker himself or herself or another person or persons speak in English (or the vernacular). This is taken to be the interpretation. It is the community which judges its genuineness, and this again is usually implied by peace, joy and love which are produced in the hearts of people. Naturally, if two or three people receive the same interpretation, or an image consonant with the interpretation is received, the community feels more assured. Father Kilian McDonnell ("Holy Spirit and Pentecostalism," *Commonweal*, 89, no. 6 1968, pp. 198–204) has sketched recent psychological research which, although it cannot judge spiritual things (cf. 1 Cor. 2), at least shows that those who possess the gift of tongues are very normal people.

(5) *Prophecy*

This service for the community is known as "prophecy in tongues." Prophecy may be given in tongues or in the vernacular. It is most important to realize that prophecy does not necessarily imply prediction. Prophecy is a *forth*telling, not a *fore*-telling, and it may be akin to the utterance of wisdom and knowledge of which St. Paul speaks (in 1 Cor. 12, 8). It is difficult to remember the exact words of prophecies (in this way they differ from audible locutions) but let us take three examples. These are not verbatim but the gist of the exhortation received.

1. "Be like a tree swaying with his will, rooted in his strength, reaching up to his love and light."

2. (Given in tongues by a Roman Catholic and interpreted by a Protestant.) "As the Holy Spirit came down upon Mary and Jesus was formed within her, so the Holy Spirit comes upon you and Jesus is in your midst."

3. "The feet of him who walked the streets of Jerusalem are behind you. His gaze is healing to those who draw near but death to those who flee." (This became very meaningful to a member in the next few days.)

The present writer does not know of any specific prediction given at a prayer meeting of Catholics. A great deal of prayer and prudent judgment would be needed if one were to take a particular line of action after a prophecy. Prophecies are intended to encourage one *generally* in the Christian life. Over-interpretation of literal understanding can be dangerous.

A prophet or prophetess needs much faith and courage to pronounce the prophecy. Very often the Holy Spirit just gives a few words; these keep recurring to the recipient with persistency, and if he or she speaks these the rest of the message may come. Frequently the recipient does not understand the sense of the sentence, but when it is given the community, further scripture readings, prophecies or images may cast light upon it. One should weigh what is said (1 Cor. 14, 31–33) and try to remember the message to help one during the week. However, let us repeat, one should not over-interpret.

(6) *Silence*

Silence is a very important part of the prayer meetings, for one must listen as well as speak to God. Silence in prayer is one of the chief characteristics of a good Catholic prayer meeting.

We have written at length about the charismatic gifts because these may not be so well known to our readers. However we must add that there is plenty, indeed, a great preponderance of informal spontaneous prayer, some formal prayers such as the Our Father, and also singing of hymns. The meeting also includes "giving of testimony." This means sharing one's religious experience (except the most intimate), for example, the overcoming of temptation, answers to prayers for both spiritual and material needs, counsels one has learned from other people, new insights into scripture, the sacraments or the truths of the Church.

Finally, two questions may be asked about these meetings. Why are the prayer meetings important? Instead of sharing religious experience, should it not be kept secret or even not "indulged in" at all?

Both these answers are found in the doctrine of the Mystical Body of Christ. Prayer meetings are community contemplation in the strictest sense of the word. Each individual has a part to play in the great orchestra of prayer and praise. In the prayer meeting one sees the fulfillment of St. Paul's teaching: "For just as the body is one and has many members, and all the members of the body, though many, are one body, so it is with Christ. For by one Spirit we were all baptized into one body—Jews or Greeks, slaves or free—and all were made to drink of one Spirit" (1 Cor. 12, 12–13).

This quotation is important because it means that everyone, *regardless* of sex, age, nationality, or even religious difference, should be allowed to follow the inspiration of the Holy Spirit. When everyone plays his or her part, one with a spontaneous prayer, another with a reading, tongue, prophecy, image or testimony, the Holy Spirit seems to build up a kind of mosaic or tapestry until a whole picture or theme often happens), so the priest is officially given by the Church the power of spiritually healing those who ask for it with the right dispositions. Just as Jesus healed the paralyzed man, a new life flowing into his body, so the priest heals the penitent and new spiritual life flows into his soul. But the sacrament should certainly be a community prayer experience.

Penance as a Prayer Meeting Using the Higher Gifts

Here is a replica of the larger prayer meeting. The minister and his "patient" pray together for an outpouring of the Holy Spirit, a release or absolution from the obstacles which quench the Holy Spirit in the spiritual patient. Truly Our Lord's words "Where two are gathered together there am I . . ." are fully realized. One should not be surprised if God uses prophecy either through the penitent or the confessor. One should expect "inspired preaching" and, occasionally, quite extraordinary things may happen. One priest was suddenly inspired to recite verbatim a passage from Ezekiel which he had read two weeks before, and this passage gave the penitent the precise counsel he needed. Another priest stretched out his hand to give absolution and his penitent was "baptized in the Spirit." Often, as the confessor speaks, the one being counselled recalls some prophecy he has received in prayer.

The Higher Gifts

Many confessors, Philip Neri for example, and probably the Curé d'Ars, brought into full play in the community sacrament of penance the gifts of counsel, wisdom, and piety as well as discernment of spirits. One should always pray that the minister and the penitent will make full use of these baptismal gifts, for here the spiritual ministries may be much more efficacious than at a prayer meeting.

For example, one uses wisdom when one is able to place all the vicissitudes of one's life, one's feelings and one's hopes, into an eternal perspective, and to see everything in proportion. Receiving the sacrament is like standing on a hill and looking at the landscape, seeing everything lying perfectly in perspective, in God's perspective. If one is down in the valley, one sees things out of proportion. In the same way, in the reception of the sacrament one is able to stand, as it were, beside God and to see oneself as God sees him and to try to remain united to his will in this respect. Although the sacrament is not primarily concerned with spiritual counsel, it is more efficacious when the two are combined, and one should be willing to share one's religious experience with the priest. It is then, very often, that the gift of understanding is utilized.

But, above all, the highest gift of the Holy Spirit, the gift of love, is the one which God most desires in the sacrament of penance. He desires this both from priest and penitent. To bring all one's failings to Our Lord, to place them at his feet, and to petition in the sacrament for the virtues which are the opposite to the vices one possesses and an expression of sorrow, deep sorrow that one has quenched the Holy Spirit given by Jesus, is a great act of love, pleasing to God, as pleasing as he found the repentance of the woman who poured the perfume over his feet, and it rejoices not only God himself but also members of the Mystical Body. The liturgical readings for the feast of Mary Magdalene are very instructive in this sense. In this sacrament we can be certain that we shall ask and receive, seek and find, knock and it will be opened to us. It is with this great expectancy of faith that we must presume that God will answer our petitionary prayer for union with him in the way that he desires.

But there is one more aspect to the prayer experience in the sacrament of penance. It is a way in which one can to some extent repair harm that one has done to other members of Christ's body, even where it is not possible to repair this on the earthly level. Thus the sacrament is an efficacious way of building up the body of Christ.

Healing of Memories

The sacrament of penance can do more than heal present sins. Often within us there are deep roots of bitterness caused by some trauma in the past. So we can ask Our Lord and Our Lady to come with us and to walk into a person's past. We know that for God the past, present and future are all one—eternity. He can change things in the past which are ordinarily beyond our control, things that are really unchangeable by human standards but which he can change. If, for example, a person's parents did not show enough love, if he or she felt rejected at an early age and felt a huge, aching void which could not be filled by any love that comes after, we can ask Our Lord to take that trial, to fill that void.

We do this in as positive a way as possible, using the imagination as much as possible, trying to picture all the details that we know about, things that happened in the past, picturing Our Lord actually healing these ills. We may actually go back to the time of birth just in case there is a memory connected with that or even before that, something picked up from the parents. Doctors tell us that even before a child can talk, he realizes very quickly what his parents think, whether he is wanted or not. He picks this up by a kind of osmosis, and perhaps this is the kind of thing that needs to be healed.

So with a prayer embodying our full imagination, not just picturing the hurt but picturing the persons standing up healed as a child or whenever it was, we pray in a spontaneous way. After that, we offer thanks that healing has taken place. If the memory has actually been healed, the person can think back to those memories which previously had been almost impossible to think about without pain and sorrow, and he can think about them with joy. There is a completely different emotional tone connected with that memory, and it is changed by Jesus.

This is a remarkable thing. Our friends have talked to people who have had wounds of the past healed, and they actually can think back to things which perhaps previously they couldn't even afford to think about, which they had repressed. Thus, penance brings the resurrection power which heals mind, body, and soul.

The power of confession extends far further than most priests and ministers realize. It extends beyond just spiritual sins to the healing of all those things connected with sin—homosexuality for example, or sometimes alcoholism. What praying in tongues or the "baptism of the Spirit" does not heal might be healed in confession. However, prayer, love, discernment of spirits, lively faith and humble, objective examination of conscience are needed.

The Sacrament of Unction

Among non-Roman Catholic Christians there are many people gifted with the ministry of healing. One thinks, for example, of Kathryn Kuhlmann and Leroy Jenkins. These people have a wonderful apostolate from Our Lord. They follow in the steps of many Roman Catholic charismatics. One very good example of a Roman Catholic with a great ministry of healing is Brother André, who established the shrine of St. Joseph in Montreal—there is plenty of literature about him.

The Roman Catholic Church does not frown upon the ministry of healing, but she is very cautious about it. Healing has always been one of God's great gifts to the Church, and miracles, usually those of healing, are required for the canonization of saints. The Church has fully approved the devotion at Lourdes. However there are dangers in the use of this gift from God. It can attract great attention; crowds may come merely to be healed rather than to give their life to Christ. It does present the possibility of certain people becoming cult heroes or heroines; there is great room for fiction or even action by the devil producing healings; there is a risk of forgetting the Giver and looking only for the gift.

Sometimes, also, there is a lack of appreciation of the role of the cross for the Christian. We must never forget that we are baptized into the suffering as well as the resurrection of Christ. There is space for a wide divergence of opinion about the place of suffering for Christians. Some people hold that God does not wish us to have any physical sufferings, such as disease, pain or illness. Others hold that one can use suffering for the greater glory of God. It would seem that suffering of some kind is almost inescapable for a Christian who wishes to unite himself or herself completely to the crucified Lord. Therefore, even if one believes that God does not wish us to have physical illness, it is to be expected that other crosses and sufferings will come into our lives. We must take these and create something good and wonderful from them.

As regards the ministry of healing, it is perhaps best to avoid many dangers by following the ministry of healing as it is performed in the Roman Catholic Church. There has been a new emphasis on the sacrament of unction. Once again, this sacrament should be administered with a lively expectation that God will heal the recipient. At the present time the sacrament can be administered even if there is only the *beginning* of the danger of death. But there are other sacramentals which the Church uses in asking for the gift of healing. These are found in the rituals. Very often, invocation of saints or even the veneration of relics(!) may be the cause of healing for many people. Even though one may not particularly like these practices, God may sometimes require an act of humility and love and ask us to do very simple and rather ridiculous looking things in order that he may give us greater graces. Therefore we should not despise these little things.

If we can attribute healing to the sacraments or sacramentals of the Church or to the charismatic leaders now residing in heaven, then we can avoid many of the dangers inherent in the great ministry of healing. Further, perhaps it is better to exercise the gift of healing very quietly and to ask people first to pray for healing from the eucharist and in the other ways described, or let the prayers for healing come quite spontaneously among prayers for other petitions. Nowadays, in this time of inter-personal relationships, people often gather together around their friends, place their hands on their heads and pray for various intentions which they have in mind—and healing can be one of these. While many incidents of healing have occurred within Catholic pentecostal groups, God does not seem to wish at the moment to raise up great healers.

One wonderful non-Roman Catholic Christian made a very wise remark. He said that he thought many non-Roman Catholic pentecostals had been given great missions of healing and attracting non-Christians by their miraculous gifts, but then it was the work of the Roman Catholic Church to deepen the spirituality of these converts and help them to use the higher gifts of wisdom, understanding, coun-sel and—especially—delicate love, and to deepen their prayer life. He said, "We are the bulldozers, you grow the seed." Perhaps he is right.

Persistency in Prayer

The Christian's vocation is to pray. But the spir-itual life is rather like physical life: if it is under-nourished it will wither and die. One needs a real dedication to the spiritual life, especially the prayer aspect and deeds of loving kindness toward one's

47

neighbor, just as one needs a dedication, for example, to music or football. One needs practice and exercise every day, otherwise one grows less proficient. There is also an analogy we can use from the married life. If a husband and wife see very little of each other and communicate very little, their love begins to grow cold. One cannot always live in the honeymoon of a spiritual life. Very often, as exuberant joy dies down, temptations, despair, trials and aridity in prayer and even falling into grave sin may follow.

No Certainty of Salvation

We can never be certain of our salvation, and herein we differ from many non-Roman Catholic Christians: Never until we reach heaven can we be certain that we are saved. St. John says that the truth is not in him who says that he has no sin. Therefore, we must work out our salvation with fear and trembling, as scripture says. Consequently, it is quite a good plan to have a certain amount of time which one sets aside for God each day, just as members of cursillo groups do. If one wants a very close union with God, it is doubtful whether less than an hour and a half or two hours of prayer a day is sufficient. One may not be called to a very close union with God. One, however, should devote a certain time to attending Mass, reading the scriptures, practicing mental prayer, and, especially, listening to God. It is very helpful to pray with other people, and, although one must not fall back into mechanical prayer, it is often useful to use formal prayer from time to time. A very efficacious form of contemplative prayer is the rosary. The rosary, however, might perhaps be said slowly, and sometimes interspersed with spontaneous prayer between the "Hail, Marys." Many people nowadays despise the rosary, but this is because it is a mature prayer that some are not ready for.

Above all, when one is drawn to rest in God's presence in silence, one should make the most of this and remain united to God in wordless prayer. One must not forget that many of the traditional devotions, such as the stations of the cross or the various litanies which have been written, were possibly written under the inspiration of the Holy Spirit. Perhaps "someone who had been baptized in the Spirit" wrote down those liturgies, those prayers. They were meaningful at the time to the authors and to other people with whom they communed in prayer. They may not be useful to us nowadays, but on the other hand they may, and we must not close our minds to any form of devotion which is approved by the Church. If God is drawing one to close union, one must expect grave temptations and trials by which he will be purified.

Respect for Other Christians

As we attempt to draw closer to Christ, we should find that we grow in humility and realize more and more our own weaknesses and inconsistency and, above all, realize that others are better than we are. We cannot expect to be perfect. Very often God sends great temptations and even allows us to fall into obvious sins in order to increase our humility, our dependence, and our love toward him. The present writer remembers a beautiful prophecy which stated that God leaves us in weakness because if he left us in strength we would not constantly return to him. This does not mean that we must despair about our sins but rather that we should not get discouraged and, especially, that we should not consider that the charismatic gifts make us special individuals within the Church in the eyes of God. Thus, keeping close to God and remembering humility, we will not fall into the Montanist mistakes of speaking of ourselves as "Spirit-filled," for no one is "Spirit-filled" except Jesus and his Blessed Mother.

And people may be inspired by the Spirit in different ways, some in very secret ways, for example a very spiritual mother who shows great love— the highest gift of the Holy Spirit—toward God and her children. Others may be inspired by the Spirit in a more dramatic way, such as being given the gift of healing. But we must not overlook those with the more hidden gifts of the Spirit. We must not speak as though other people are not baptized in the Spirit and, especially, we must not see the prayer gift of the gift of tongues as a necessary sign that people are baptized in the Holy Spirit. Indeed, the very phrase "baptized in the Spirit" is misleading because it might lead people to think that they did not receive the Holy Spirit in the sacrament of baptism and that they did not continue to receive him in a special way in confirmation and the eucharist. This would be diametrically opposed to Catholic doctrine. Catholics have always resolutely maintained that the prime source of the Holy Spirit is in the sacraments of baptism and confirmation, culminating in the totality of the experience which is received in the eucharist. Therefore, it is better to use a phrase such as "awakening of the Spirit" or "release of the Spirit."

It is also better to avoid very demonstrative or emotional behavior. There is nothing wrong with it, and one who is inspired by the Spirit should be full of joy, but one should also be sensitive to others. Culturally, many people do not accept demonstrative behavior. Therefore, dancing in the Spirit, gesturing with one's hands or raising the voice in frequent "Praise the Lord," "Alleluia" or other kinds of behavior may turn people away (cf. 1 Cor. 8, 7–13; 9, 19–23). One must also try to avoid turning "testimonies" into "success stories." One must bear in mind that it is always God who moves, and it is good to report some of our failings as well as some of God's successes. Sensitivity to other people's feelings is "love."

51

Other Innocent but Misleading Terms

Sometimes we speak about "praying over some-one." It is better to say "praying for someone." This is just a different form of petitionary prayer. We pray for someone but in his presence with a human gesture by putting one's hands on the head or shoul-der of the person for whom we pray. This outward gesture is merely an external manifestation of our interior disposition, that of faith and supporting love. We who are weak in faith need external manifesta-tion. But speaking about praying "over people" or "laying hands on people" gives the wrong impression and sounds like "magic"; it sets up certain tensions and fears within people. We should not be dramatic about this but merely see this type of praying for someone rather in the order of shaking hands in the social dimension.

Further, when we speak about being *baptized in the Spirit,* we must not forget that the Holy Spirit is present in the world and indwelling in every person sacramentally baptized, waiting for a response from that person. This prayer experience means that the presence of the Holy Spirit is made even more effi-cacious, is unleashed, and the person becomes con-scious of being immersed in the love of the Holy Spirit. But even if one does not feel the Holy Spirit, he is still present. We must never speak about some-one being without the Holy Spirit if he or she has no actual experience. What counts is faith and the fact that he is baptized. The Spirit has always been there since sacramental baptism, but he is a Person and does not work without an invitation. We should also make it quite obvious to our friends that we are conscious of a variety of modality. The Holy Spirit can come in the way that he wishes. Praying for someone with the human gesture of placing hands on his head is not the only way. Never let anyone feel out of place if he disagrees with this practice or if he does not possess "tongues." *Never* speak about "we" and "they"—the Montanists did that.

Many people speak about *laying a claim on the Lord* or *asking in the name of the Lord*. Some people insist that we should not insert the clause "if it is your will," but rather that we should expect God to answer our prayer whatever it is. The present writer does not feel that this is in accordance with experience or with the deepest spirituality. God has more wisdom than he or she who prays, and to ask in the name of God means that we ask according to the "character" (that is what "name" means in the Hebrew sense) of Jesus, whose meat and drink it was to do the will of him who sent him. If we pray for anything which is in the character of Jesus, we can be certain that the prayer will be answered: for example, deliverance from sins and spiritual benefits, but not necessarily physical or material benefits. We must also recall that while Jesus asked his Father to take away the chalice in the garden of

53

Gethsemane, he added that he wished his Father's will to be done, not his own. There does seem to be a little bit of vanity or sentimentality and rather a lot of selfishness if we expect God to answer every prayer that we offer, so we must be discerning. Let us not "organize" God.

"In the same way, we must use the gift of discernment, if we *"place a fleece before the Lord."* This means that we ask for a sign from God. For example, we might say "If you wish me to do such and such a thing, let such and such a thing happen." But we must be careful that there is no selfishness intermingled with our intent, and we must be careful not to misinterpret the sign. In important matters it is always better to do this very, very prayerfully in the group and let the matter be adjudicated by the community.

Many people speak about *an anointing from the Lord*. This appears to mean a certain feeling, and sometimes a powerful feeling, within them. Some people feel burning in their hands or even some sensation between the shoulders. It would appear that the Holy Spirit is impeded rather than helped by too much emotional behavior. Although these anointings may be quite genuine, they do not seem to be absolutely necessary, and we must be careful that they do not arise from a psychological need or from a need of self-identity. Let us be perfectly calm and peaceful and look at the interior rather than the exterior happenings.

Many people nowadays think it more sophisticated to deny the existence of the *devil* or *evil spirits*. To those people we can say only that it is difficult to believe what you have not experienced, but it is equally difficult not to believe what one has experienced. Those who have worked in the missions or had experience with deeply spiritual people know that when the Holy Spirit is working very efficaciously, evil spirits or the devil often make direct attacks or are very active in certain insidious ways.

Nevertheless, one must be careful indeed not to talk much about the devil or to misdiagnose cases where there is a psychological upset rather than obsession. Talking about devils is misleading and frightening for an outsider, and very few people can be certain of really discerning the action of an evil spirit from other psychological disturbances. Nevertheless, although prayers of exorcism are very often quite helpful, again let them be done in calmness and quiet, without ostentation and drama. Certainly, we must not say that physical disease is due to devils; this is a primitive way of thinking.

We must say a word about the *interpretation of scripture*. It is quite clear that the pentecostal movement has drawn people to scripture. Many who denied the action of the supernatural before, claiming for example that the miracles in the New Testament were fiction, legends composed by the writers, are now drawn to see the truth in scripture, accepting the historicity of the scriptures. They accept the birth, life, death and resurrection of Jesus and the charismatic occurrences in the early Church (and the modern Church) as real events.

This is not to be confused with fundamentalism. Fundamentalism interprets the bible quite literally, and this can be a source of serious misinterpretation of scripture. For example, if we took Genesis 1–11 or the Apocalypse of St. John quite literally, we would be in great trouble. What we must do is to integrate good and sure academic progress in biblical scholarship with spirituality, and accept nothing which is inconsistent with the small body of defined dogma of the Church, for example denying three Persons in One God.

One very widespread error is the identification of the pentecostal Catholic movement with *sensitivity groups* and *group dynamics!* Nothing could be further from the truth! Indeed, Catholic pentecostals do meet together for prayer, but the meetings are completely unstructured and completely divorced from psychological dynamics. Further, in pentecostal groups, one speaks about the activity of God rather than the actions of other people.

Unfortunately, a few Catholics have made a dreadful mistake and have accepted *re-baptism* within some non-Roman Catholic Churches. The non-Roman Catholics are not, of course, to be blamed, and perhaps the Catholics were not well instructed, yet, this is a very grave mistake and must be displeasing to Our Lord. Catholics were truly baptized with water and the Holy Spirit in the sacrament of baptism. The amount of water, whether it was a few drops poured over a baby's forehead or total immersion, does not matter to the Holy Spirit; what matters is the giving of the Holy Spirit and the new creature who is born of this sacrament. What we call the release of the Holy Spirit is full Christianity and a way of life, often accompanied by certain extraordinary charismata. But these extraordinary charismata are not absolutely necessary; certainly they are not necessary for salvation. The "baptism of the Spirit" gives the experience of a new dimension of spiritual life with new power and maturity.

One other precaution that we should take is not to become *"pushy pentecostals."* God may not desire everyone to have the same experience, since the whole doctrine of the body of Christ presupposes that we have different gifts and different functions, yet are equal. Therefore we should speak with discretion and joy about God's own gifts to us, leaving other people quite free to join prayer groups if they so wish. Above all, we must never, never give the idea that we are better Christians than others. God does seem to have given these charismatic gifts in greater abundance, possibly to help the ecumenical movement.

The work of the Holy Spirit is twofold: the transformation of the individual and the unification of mankind. Through the pentecostal experience many Christians of various persuasions are drawn together in greater love and greater understanding. Catholics can humbly say they have received many things from their contact with non-Roman Catholics, but non-Roman Catholics equally acknowledge that they are beginning to understand our doctrine more, even having veneration for the eucharist and the Virgin Mary. However the Holy Spirit works in many different ways in the Church. The pentecostal apostolate is only one of these.

Conclusion

The avoidance of these mistakes will enhance our apostolic activity. The apostolic activity is the ministry of love of which St. Paul speaks. No one has given a better description of love than St. Thomas Aquinas; he called it *diffisium sui*. This is exactly Jesus' idea of love. When he ascended into heaven—that is, when he exercised the fullness of his kingship and his priesthood—he sent down gifts or responsibilities of the Holy Spirit to the Church, so that by diffusing, as it were, his own nature by grace, the Church could reflect his own person by the gifts which he had given her. The author of the Epistle to the Ephesians says: "I . . . beg you to live a life worthy of the calling to which you have been called, with all lowliness and meekness, with patience for bearing one another in love, eager to maintain the unity of the Spirit, the bond of peace. There is one body and one Spirit, just as